CONTENTS

FORGIVING WHAT YOU CAN'T FORGET

DISCOVER HOW TO MOVE ON, MAKE PEACE
WITH PAINFUL MEMORIES, AND CREATE A LIFE
THAT'S BEAUTIFUL AGAIN

STUDY GUIDE · · · SIX SESSIONS

LYSA TERKEURST

NELSON
BOOKS

An Imprint of Thomas Nelson

Published in Nashville, Tennessee, by Nelson Books, an imprint of Thomas Nelson. Nelson Books and Thomas Nelson are registered trademarks of HarperCollins Christian Publishing, Inc.

Thomas Nelson titles may be purchased in bulk for educational, business, fund-raising, or sales promotional use. For information, please e-mail SpecialMarkets@ThomasNelson.com.

Scripture quotations, unless otherwise noted, are taken from the Holy Bible, New International Version®, NIV®. Copyright © 1973, 1978, 1984, 2011 by Biblica, Inc.® Used by permission of Zondervan. All rights reserved worldwide. www .Zondervan.com. The "NIV" and "New International Version" are trademarks registered in the United States Patent and Trademark Office by Biblica, Inc.®

Scripture quotations marked AMP are from the Amplified® Bible. Copyright © 1954, 1958, 1962, 1964, 1965, 1987 by The Lockman Foundation. Used by permission. (www.Lockman.org)

Scripture quotations marked ESV are from the ESV® Bible (The Holy Bible, English Standard Version®). Copyright © 2001 by Crossway, a publishing ministry of Good News Publishers. Used by permission. All rights reserved.

Scripture quotations marked THE MESSAGE are from *The Message*. Copyright © by Eugene H. Peterson 1993, 1994, 1995, 1996, 2000, 2001, 2002. Used by permission of NavPress. All rights reserved. Represented by Tyndale House Publishers, Inc.

Scripture quotations marked NKJV are taken from the New King James Version®. © 1982 by Thomas Nelson. Used by permission. All rights reserved.

Scripture quotations marked NLT are from the Holy Bible, New Living Translation®. © 1996, 2004, 2007, 2013, 2015 by Tyndale House Foundation. Used by permission of Tyndale House Publishers, Inc., Carol Stream, Illinois 60188. All rights reserved.

Any Internet addresses, phone numbers, or company or product information printed in this book are offered as a resource and are not intended in any way to be or to imply an endorsement by Thomas Nelson, nor does Thomas Nelson vouch for the existence, content, or services of these sites, phone numbers, companies, or products beyond the life of this book.

ISBN 978-0-310-10486-5 (softcover)
ISBN 978-0-310-10494-0 (ebook)

First Printing October 2020 / Printed in the United States of America

Hi, friend.

I'm so grateful you decided to join me for this study about forgiving what we can't forget. I'm also proud of you. Because I know deeply and personally how hard all of this can be.

When your heart has been shattered and reshaped into something that doesn't quite feel normal inside your own chest, forgiveness can feel so very unrealistic.

At first, we say it's too soon.

And then years go by, and we say it's too late.

In my own life, I knew as a Christian I was supposed to forgive. I may have even whispered a faint prayer using the word *forgiveness*. But truly understanding how to forgive? I wasn't sure. And isn't it odd that, though forgiveness is a major part of the Christian faith, most of us have never been taught much about it?

We know God commands us to do it. But how? Why? When? And are there exceptions?

After nearly a thousand hours of studying this topic in the Bible, I can't say all my questions have been answered. Nor can I promise this is easy. But I can tell you the Bible offers the truth about forgiveness that our souls desperately need. And, best of all, God Himself modeled how to do this even when it feels impossible.

Instead of digging into just one book of the Bible during this study, we'll be looking at incredibly rich passages throughout Scripture. These truths have meant so much to me personally in my own journey with forgiveness, and I'm believing they're going to leave you forever changed too.

So, let's open up His Word, open up our hearts, and invite His healing in.

Together, we can start seeing beautiful again.

*Forgiveness
is a complicated*
GRACE
*that uncomplicates
my blinding pain
and helps me see*
BEAUTIFUL
again.

HOW TO USE THIS GUIDE

GROUP SIZE

The *Forgiving What You Can't Forget* video study is designed to be experienced in a group setting, such as a Bible study, Sunday school class, or any small group gathering. To ensure everyone has enough time to participate in discussion, larger groups can break up into smaller circles of four to six people after the video is viewed. If you do need to split into smaller groups during your class time, make sure to select one person in each group to act as a facilitator for that group during your discussion.

MATERIALS NEEDED

Each participant should have her own copy of this study guide, as well as her own copy of the book *Forgiving What You Can't Forget*. This study guide contains notes for video segments, discussion questions, and personal studies that will deepen learning between group sessions. In addition, the leader will need to have the videos either on DVD or by digital stream/download.

WEEKLY SCHEDULE

This study guide also provides information at the beginning of each week on which chapters of the book should be read before the group session. You will dig deeper into the book in the personal studies between group sessions. *Please note: It is recommended that the participants read the introduction and chapters 1–2 before the first class.*

Below is a sample of the schedule you will find at the beginning of every new week.

BEFORE GROUP MEETING	Read Chapters _____ *Forgiving What You Can't Forget* Book
GROUP MEETING	View Video Session ____ : _____ Group Discussion Pages _____
PERSONAL STUDY DAY 1	Pages _____
PERSONAL STUDY DAY 2	Pages _____
PERSONAL STUDY DAY 3	Pages _____
DAYS 4 & 5 BEFORE WEEK _____ GROUP MEETING	Read Chapters _____ *Forgiving What You Can't Forget* Book Complete Any Unfinished Personal Study Activities

TIMING

Time notations have been given for each heading of the group meeting sections of the study. These indicate the *actual* time of the video segments and the *suggested times* for discussion.

Noting these times will help you to complete each session within the time frame your group has available. If your group meets for two hours, you will most likely be able to cover a majority of the questions. Feel free to use any extra time you may have to go back and look at the previous week's homework together, discussing the chapters and study questions more in depth. If your group meets for 90 minutes, you may find you need to pick a few of your favorite group questions to discuss after the video. Remember, the ultimate goal isn't to make it through every single question but to have beneficial and meaningful discussions. We've found some of the most profound moments of a Bible study can happen when participants share experiential wisdom and personal revelations with one another.

You may also opt to devote two meetings rather than one to each session. In addition to allowing conversations to be more spacious, this option has the added advantage of allowing time to discuss the personal studies and the chapters of the book. In the second meeting for each session, devote the time usually allotted for watching the video to discussing participants' insights and questions from their reading and personal study.

FACILITATION

Each group should appoint a facilitator who is responsible for starting the video and for keeping track of time during discussions. Facilitators may also read questions aloud and monitor discussions, prompting participants to respond and ensuring that everyone has an opportunity to participate. A brief leader's guide for each session can be found in the back of this study guide.

Schedule

WEEK 1

BEFORE GROUP MEETING	Read Introduction and Chapters 1–2 *Forgiving What You Can't Forget* Book
GROUP MEETING	View Video Session 1: What Am I Supposed to Do With All the Hurt? Group Discussion Pages 12–18
PERSONAL STUDY DAY 1	Pages 19–24
PERSONAL STUDY DAY 2	Pages 24–29
PERSONAL STUDY DAY 3	Pages 30–36
DAYS 4 & 5 BEFORE WEEK 2 GROUP MEETING	Read Chapters 3–4 *Forgiving What You Can't Forget* Book Complete Any Unfinished Personal Study Activities

WHAT AM I SUPPOSED TO DO WITH ALL THE *Hurt?*

SESSION 1

WELCOME! (SUGGESTED TIME: 2-5 MINUTES)

Welcome to session 1 of *Forgiving What You Can't Forget*. If this is your first time together as a group, take a moment to introduce yourselves to one another before watching the video. Then let's get started!

OPENING REFLECTION: (SUGGESTED TIME: 10-15 MINUTES)

Leader Note: Have a few people share their response to this question before starting the video:

What was your most helpful takeaway from the introduction or chapters 1-2 of the book?

VIDEO (25:30 MINUTES)

Leader Note: Play the video segment for the Introduction and Session 1.

> ## THIS WEEK'S STATEMENT TO HOLD ONTO:
>
> Forgiveness is not made possible by our determination. Forgiveness is made possible by our cooperation with what God has already done for us.

VIDEO NOTES

Use the outline below to help you follow along with the teaching video or to take additional notes on anything that stands out.

Forgiveness and reconciliation are not a package deal.

Forgiveness is the very thing God designed to help heal the hurting human heart.

When we refuse to let God's forgiveness flow through us to other people, it becomes a heavy weight that can cause anxiety, fear, depression and angst that no human should have to bear.

Forgiveness isn't dependent on another person making this right. It's between me and God.

Genesis 4:1–7: The story of Cain and Abel

> v. 6 paraphrase: "Cain, why are you heating up all of your worries and frustrations to the point you are filled with anxiety and depression?"

Psalm 4:4:

> "Be angry, and do not sin;
> > ponder in your own hearts on your beds, and be silent." (ESV)

Psalm 36:1–4: ". . . even on their beds they plot evil." (v. 4)

Psalm 36:5–10

> v. 5: "Your love, Lord, reaches to the heavens,
>   your faithfulness to the skies."

The more we focus on God, the more focused we are on His peace. The more we focus on His peace, the more we'll feel His peace.

When I only think I need a little bit of God's forgiveness flowing to me, then I'm only willing to let very little forgiveness flow through me.

Matthew 5:42–44 (The Message Translation) "And if someone takes unfair advantage of you, use the occasion to practice the servant life . . . love your enemies. Let them bring out the best in you, not the worst." (v. 42)

Genesis 4:7: "If you do what is right" = "To make a thing good, or right, or beautiful."[1]

Forgiveness is a complicated grace that uncomplicates my anger and helps me see beautiful again.

Group DISCUSSION

(Suggested time: 40–45 minutes)

Leader Note: We have suggested questions to start with, but feel free to pick any of the additional questions as well. Consider the timeframe of your group and know the ultimate goal is meaningful discussion.

Please know there is no shame or condemnation as you answer these questions. Remember, this is just the beginning of a journey that will be beneficial, but also hard at times.

SUGGESTED QUESTIONS

1. It's not uncommon for people to pull back and want to self-protect when they hear the word *forgiveness*. What are some of the reasons we may feel resistant to the idea of forgiveness?

2. In today's video we learned that forgiveness isn't made possible by our determination. Forgiveness is made possible by our cooperation with what God has already done for us. What do you think it means to cooperate with what God has already done?

3. Before watching this video, did you think that forgiveness and reconciliation were always a package deal? Why is it still important to forgive someone even if we don't reconcile our relationship with them?

4. Have someone read Genesis 4:6–8 aloud. God asks Cain to pull back from all the emotion swirling inside of him and to choose to do the right and good thing. What does Cain do instead? While most people would never go so far as murder, what could be some of the devastating outcomes of refusing to allow God to address feelings of anger, anxiety, and despair in our own lives? Why is it important to process forgiveness using God's Word instead of only our thoughts and feelings?

ADDITIONAL QUESTIONS (as time allows)

5. Read 1 Peter 5:7–9 aloud: "Cast all your anxiety on him because he cares for you. Be alert and of sober mind. Your enemy the devil prowls around like a roaring lion looking for someone to devour. Resist him, standing firm in the faith, because you know that the family of believers throughout the world is undergoing the same kind of sufferings."

What similarities do you see between this warning and the one God gives Cain at the end of Genesis 4:7: ". . . sin is crouching at your door; it desires to have you, but you must rule over it"?

6. Open your Bible to Psalm 36:1-4. Read this passage aloud and then discuss the attributes of someone who gives in to sin instead of ruling over it. Which of these descriptions do you find personally convicting?

7. Now read Psalm 36:5-10 aloud, changing readers every few verses. What attributes of God do we find in this passage that can help us quiet those things that make us anxious about forgiveness? List as many as you can.

8. We learned today that forgiveness is a complicated grace that uncomplicates our anger and helps us see beautiful again. What are some ways unforgiveness can keep us from seeing beauty in our lives? How could forgiveness help us start seeing beautiful again?

CLOSING (SUGGESTED TIME: 5-MINUTES)

Leader Note: End your session by reading the "Between-Sessions Personal Studies" instructions on the next page to the group and making sure there are no questions pertaining to the homework. Then take a few minutes to pray over your group, either reading the provided prayer aloud over them or praying your own prayer.

BETWEEN-SESSIONS PERSONAL STUDIES

Every session in the *Forgiving What You Can't Forget Study Guide* includes five days of personal study to help you make meaningful connections between your life and what you're learning each week. In this first week, you'll work with the material in the introduction and chapters 1–2 of the book *Forgiving What You Can't Forget.* You'll also have time to read chapters 3–4 of the book in preparation for our next group meeting.

PRAYER

Father God, as we start this journey, we're so thankful we can trust Your love for us. And we're deeply grateful You never shame us for our struggles with forgiveness. Instead, You simply invite us to come to You for Your wisdom, help, and hope. So, that is what we're doing. Please help us to see forgiveness as a gift and not one more burden on our already broken hearts. Help us to believe that healing and freedom are possible, not just for other people but for us. And help us learn to forgive as You have forgiven us. Freely. Completely. Not to excuse what's been done to us, but to set us free. You are good. Your ways are good. And that means we can trust that forgiveness is good too. In Jesus' name, amen.

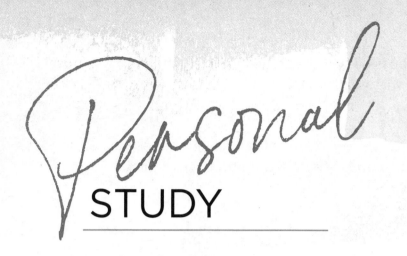

STUDY

DAY 1
STUDY AND REFLECT

Today we're going to reflect more on the video and the introduction of the book *Forgiving What You Can't Forget.* If you haven't already read the introduction, please do so before you begin.

What if?

There's something so inviting about these two words. They don't demand an answer. They don't force us to land on one side or the other of an issue. Instead, they kindly and humbly ask us to consider something we may have never truly sat with before.

What if?

What if forgiveness isn't supposed to be another hard thing we have to do? *What if* it's the necessary step to finally experience the peace we desperately want but can't seem to get any other way? *What if* forgiveness is what's been missing in all the relational chaos we're so worn out from dealing with in our lives?

These are some of the questions we'll be sitting with in this study. There's no rush to answer them or even to like them right now. There's also no judgment for any resistance we may currently be feeling toward forgiveness. God gives us full permission to show up with our most honest and vulnerable thoughts and emotions. But He also wants us to bring our willingness. A willingness to open our hearts to the possibility that forgiveness truly is one of the most healing, crucial, and beautiful gifts from Him.

Let's begin . . .

1. When you hear the word *forgiveness*, what is your gut-honest, initial response? Write down any and every word that comes to mind.

2. How free do you feel to be honest with God about your struggles with forgiveness?

——1——2——3——4——5——6——7——8——9——10——

I feel completely
free to tell
God how I feel

I am afraid God will
be disappointed in me
for my struggles

Read Psalm 62:8: "Trust in him at all times, you people; pour out your hearts to him, for God is our refuge."

How does this verse speak to your heart about talking openly with God as you work through this study?

Our God is big enough to handle our honest feelings and questions we're wrestling through. Honesty is essential for our hearts to be able to heal. Tiptoeing around pretending to be fine, fine, fine with everything that comes our way would be fake at best, deadening at worst. We can bring our gut-honest struggles to God in prayer and use His Word in Scripture to help us process them. The purpose of doing this isn't to say our feelings should lead us . . . it's actually the opposite. The purpose is to use His truth as our "filter" or "guide" so we can have a God-honoring lens through which to process our feelings. He gives us a healthier perspective. Knowing this, do you need to go back to question 1 and add anything you were hesitant to write down at first?

3. Open up your Bible, and let's revisit Genesis 4:1–7 one more time. This may seem like a small detail, but *who* approached Cain about his anger?

_____

Who is ultimately asking *us* to take a look at what is going on in us internally right now? _____

Remembering **who** is asking us to forgive is vital as we navigate forgiveness within the complexities of relationships where we've been deeply wounded. The one requesting this of us is the God who made us, loves us and has good plans for us. The God who does everything on purpose and with purpose. The God we can lean into and trust.

In what ways could knowing God is the one asking this of us soften our hearts toward the idea of forgiveness?

4. As we begin this journey, it's also important to remember God's character and attributes.

Let's read 2 Corinthians 1:3–5: "Praise be to the God and Father of our Lord Jesus Christ, the Father of compassion and the God of all comfort, who comforts us in all our troubles, so that we can comfort those in any trouble with the comfort we ourselves receive from God. For just as we share abundantly in the sufferings of Christ, so also our comfort abounds through Christ."

How is God described? A comforter, compassionate

Where have you already experienced God's comfort in your life in the midst of your trouble and pain?

Just knowing he's there for me, that he cares about me

So many times when we are deeply hurt by someone else, forgiveness can feel like another hard thing we have to do on top of trying to heal. But since God is compassionate, we can know forgiveness isn't a cruel command. Rather, forgiveness is His way of freeing us from the heavy burdens of bitterness, resentment, anger, and retaliation. In essence, forgiveness is not just for the offender but also a gracious gift to us as well. How does this help you start to shift your perspective of forgiveness?

5. Please read the book excerpt below and then answer the questions that follow.

"You can't edit reality to try and force healing. You can't fake yourself into being okay with what happened. But you can decide that the one who hurt you doesn't get to decide what you do with your memories. Your life can be a graceful combination of beautiful and painful. You don't have to put either definitive label on what once was. It can be both-and.

Maybe that's part of what's hard about moving on: the letting go. But what if it's possible to let go of what we must but still carry with us what is beautiful and meaningful and true to us? And maybe this less-severe version of moving on is what will ease us to a place of forgiveness." (*Forgiving What You Can't Forget*, pages XVI–XVIII)

Do you ever have times where you try to force yourself to just feel better or to get over what happened? Do you ever worry God wants you to just hurry up and be done with all of this hurting? Or, do you find yourself clinging to the hurt and fear, believing that if you take steps to forgive, all the ways you were hurt will be too soon forgotten or unfairly glossed over? Write your thoughts.

Now read the verses below.

> "As a father has compassion on his children,
>   so the Lord has compassion on those who fear him;
> for he knows how we are formed,
>   he remembers that we are dust." **Psalm 103:13–14**

> "You keep track of all my sorrows.
>   You have collected all my tears in your bottle.
>   You have recorded each one in your book." **Psalm 56:8** (NLT)

What do these verses mean to you personally in light of the idea that we don't have to rush healing, fake being fine, or just say the words "I forgive" to check a box?

6. Read Psalm 36:5–10. What attributes of God do you need to cling to personally as you choose to trust Him throughout this process of forgiveness? Fill in the blanks below using a few of those attributes to help you hold tightly to the truth of who God is.

Thank You, God, that You are _____. Knowing this will help me _____
_____ .

Thank You, God, that You are _____. Knowing this will help me _____
_____ .

Thank You, God, that You are _____. Knowing this will help me _____
_____ .

7. Please read the book excerpt below and then finish out today with the instructions that follow.

> "It is necessary for you not to let pain rewrite your memories. And it's absolutely necessary not to let pain ruin your future." (*Forgiving What You Can't Forget*, page XVIII)

The hurt you have experienced is real, friend. But it's taken enough away from you. And your heart is much too beautiful of a place for bitterness, anger, and resentment. Finish today by reading Psalm 42:5 out loud. Let it be a personal declaration to your own soul—you *do* have hope in God. And seeing beautiful again *is* possible with Him.

> "Why, my soul, are you downcast?
>   Why so disturbed within me?
> Put your hope in God,
>   for I will yet praise him,
>   my Savior and my God." **Psalm 42:5**

DAY 2
STUDY AND REFLECT

Today we're going to reflect on chapter 1 of the book *Forgiving What You Can't Forget.* If you haven't already read chapter 1, please do so before you begin.

> ". . . when I wrongly think forgiveness rises and falls on all my efforts, mustered-up grit, conjured maturity, bossed-around resistance, and gentle feelings that feel real one moment and fake the next, I'll never be able to authentically give the kind of forgiveness Jesus has given me.
>
> My ability to forgive others rises and falls, instead, on this: leaning into what Jesus has already done, which allows His grace *for me* to flow freely *through me* (see Ephesians 4:7).

Forgiveness isn't an act of my determination.

Forgiveness is only made possible by my cooperation."
(*Forgiving What You Can't Forget*, page 7)

1. Have you been trying to muster up the strength to forgive others on your own? How does it make you feel to know He is inviting you to *join* Him in His work of forgiveness?

2. Chapter 1 lists many things this journey through forgiveness is NOT. Check the ones you are most thankful for. Circle any that actually surprised you.

Forgiveness is not a message that:

- ☐ Diminishes what you've been through or makes light of the anguish you've cried a million tears over.

- ☐ Justifies abuse or abandonment or affairs that are all wrong no matter how it's flipped or framed by others.

- ☐ Refuses to acknowledge how powerful feelings are and how powerless you can feel when you get flooded by pain, triggered by memories, ignored by those who were supposed to love you, or brushed aside by those who should have cared for you.

- ☐ Demands you excuse the cruelest and most horrific crimes committed against you or those you love.

- ☐ Gives a nod in the direction of demanding all relationships work out with all people—sometimes that's neither possible nor safe.

3. The purpose of the list above is to assure you this message is one that is overflowing with grace. But, as we learned in chapter 1, grace isn't the only thing we are going to need in order to heal.

——— GRACE ———

*unmerited favor, something that we cannot earn
but is freely given to us*

Look up John 1:14 and John 1:17 in your Bible. What two things does Scripture say Jesus showed up with?

Why do you think Jesus came with grace *and* truth?

What could be the danger of us approaching the message of forgiveness with all grace but no truth?

What are the dangers of all truth and no grace?

4. Please read the book excerpt below and then answer the questions that follow.

> "If I only offered you grace, I would be shortchanging you on what it truly takes to heal. While the truth is sometimes hard to hear, God gives it to us because He knows what our hearts and souls really need. It is His truth that sets us free." (*Forgiving What You Can't Forget*, page 6)

Freedom and healing won't be possible without the truth of God's Word. Look up each of the passages listed below and then use the space provided to write about how each one complements the idea of Scripture helping us walk in freedom and healing.

Psalm 19:7–11:

2 Timothy 3:16–17:

Hebrews 4:12:

Look back at all three of these passages. What do you feel that you most need God's Word to reveal to you right now? Wisdom? Light in your darkness? A better understanding of forgiveness? Help you rightly discern all that is going on within your heart? Something else? Write your thoughts below. Then, pause for a moment to thank God for all that He is able to accomplish in you through His Word.

FIGURING OUT FORGIVENESS

"To the Jews who had believed him,
Jesus said, 'If you hold to my teaching,
you are really my disciples. Then you
will know the truth, and the truth
will set you free.'" John 8:31-32

The Greek word for *hold* in John 8:31 is **menō**. It is a word that means "to abide, to remain." This is a critical theme that we see show up in a concentrated way in John 15.[2] George R. Beasley-Murray states in his commentary that this verb "signifies a settled determination to live in the word of Christ and by it, and so entails a perpetual listening to it, reflection on it, holding fast to it, carrying out its bidding."[3]

This is why we are processing forgiveness through the lens of Scripture. As followers of Christ, we are called to listen to the Word, reflect on the Word, hold fast to the Word, and live out the Word. This is what it means to "abide" in Christ and for Christ to be in us. And this is where freedom and fruitfulness become possible.

5. Think of one situation where you've felt as though forgiveness might be asking too much from you. What does it seem like you're giving up to forgive this person or people? What could you possibly gain from forgiving this person or people?

Giving up our right to be resentful or to seek revenge when our hearts have been deeply wounded can feel hard. Let's see what Scripture has to say, remembering that even when Scripture feels difficult, what it teaches us is always for our good.

Fill in the blanks.

"Do not repay _____ with _____ or _____ with _____. On the contrary, repay _____ with _____, because to this you were called so that you may inherit a _____." **1 Peter 3:9** (NIV)

What is your initial response to this verse? How does it feel possible or impossible in light of all that you have faced?

Read 1 Peter 2:21-23 in your Bible and then answer the questions below.

Did Jesus have every right to retaliate? Why or why not?

When are you most tempted to feel that retaliation is justifiable?

Why does this passage of Scripture say He was able to trust God instead of seeking retribution?

Do you trust God to handle things rightly, even if you never get to see how? (Please don't feel frustrated with yourself or condemned if your answer to that last question is "no." We will dive further into trusting the justice of God later in the study.)

6. In both the video and in the introduction, we've looked at how refusing to let God's forgiveness flow through us to other people can become a heavy weight that causes anxiety, fear, depression, and angst inside of us.

   Have you ever stopped to consider that unforgiveness may actually be compounding your pain? In what ways could this be playing out in your own life?

   Remembering how much forgiveness has flowed *to* us can help as we begin this process of letting it flow *through* us. Spend some time looking up these passages of Scripture. Ask the Lord to use these verses to begin softening your heart toward the idea of forgiving as you have been forgiven. Circle which one resonates with you personally, and write why in the space below.

   1 John 1:9   Colossians 2:13-15   Psalm 103:8-14   Isaiah 43:25

   End today by writing out a prayer of thanksgiving for the Lord's mercy and forgiveness.

STUDY AND REFLECT

Today we're going to reflect on chapter 2 of the book *Forgiving What You Can't Forget.* If you haven't already read chapter 2, please do so before you begin.

1. Please read the book excerpt below and then answer the questions that follow.

   "... we each wrestled through our own questions about forgiveness in the midst of the gritty, tearful, desperate experiences we brought to the table. And, though you didn't know it, we always had an extra chair for you.

   Here, your questions are safe. Your heartbreak is tenderly held. Your thoughts don't need to be edited. Your soul's need for truth will be tended to. And your resistance is understood. Welcome to the gray table, friend." (*Forgiving What You Can't Forget*, page 15)

   Psalm 23:5 reads,

   > "You prepare a table before me
   >   in the presence of my enemies.
   > You anoint my head with oil;
   >   my cup overflows."

   No matter how many tables we've been invited to or excluded from, the Lord says we always have a place at His. Stop to truly consider this. What does it mean to you that Jesus says you are always loved, always welcome, always invited near?

2. This concept of being welcomed to the table is important as we purposefully sit with this message of forgiveness over the next few weeks. In Scripture, the table is presented as a place of communion, conversation, and connectivity. It is a place we go to know others and invite others to know us. It is a space that's meant to flow with the balanced rhythm of giving and receiving.

In the Old Testament, the prophets used imagery of a great feast to represent the rule and reign of God (Isaiah 25:6). It's an image that helps us picture God inviting us to experience not only nourishment and sustenance, but also the comfort of His presence and power.

We also find Jesus sharing meals around tables in the New Testament, the most memorable being the Last Supper. This is the table Jesus shared with His disciples before He went to the cross, and it's one He invites us to still today as we take communion together in remembrance of His sacrifice for our redemption. (See Mark 14:22-25; Luke 22:18-20; 1 Corinthians 11:23-25.)

And while there are no physical tables present, there are two other moments surrounding meals and Jesus that we would be wise not to overlook. When Peter publicly denies Jesus in John 18, he is near a charcoal fire where eating and drinking were most likely taking place. It's a moment that then connects directly to another scene around a charcoal fire with Jesus and Peter in John 21, when the resurrected Jesus prepares a meal for His disciples and then publicly restores Peter. We find in the intertwining of these moments, and even in all that is represented by the Last Supper, that the table is the perfect place for the broken and battered to find redemption and restoration from the provider of the meal—Jesus.

Let's read that last line again: ". . . the table is the perfect place for the broken and battered to find redemption and restoration from the provider of the meal—Jesus."

How do these words impact you in light of this study?

Is there anything else you read in the paragraphs above that stood out to you or encouraged you?

3. Remembering that we have permission to show up to this conversation with all of our brokenness, doubts, and questions, read through the list below. These are some of the feelings that can feed our resistance to forgiveness. Do any of these resonate with you? Check the ones that apply:

1. ___ I fear the offense will be repeated.
2. ___ Hanging on to a grudge gives me a sense of control in a situation that's felt so unfair.
3. ___ The pain I experienced altered my life, and yet no one has ever validated that what I went through was wrong.
4. ___ Forgiveness feels like it trivializes, minimizes, or, worse yet, makes what happened no big deal.
5. ___ I can't possibly forgive when I still feel so hostile toward the one who hurt me.
6. ___ I'm not ready to forgive.
7. ___ I still feel hurt.
8. ___ They haven't apologized or even acknowledged that what they did was wrong.
9. ___ Being back in relationship with this person isn't possible or safe. Furthermore, it's not even reasonable for me to have a conversation with the person who hurt me.
10. ___ I'm still in the middle of a long, hard situation with no resolution yet.
11. ___ I'm afraid forgiveness will give them false hope that I want to reestablish the relationship, but I don't.
12. ___ It's easier to ignore this person altogether than to try to figure out boundaries so they don't keep hurting me.
13. ___ What they did is unchangeable; therefore, forgiveness won't help anything.
14. ___ The person who hurt me is no longer here. I can't forgive someone I can't talk to.
15. ___ I don't think any good will come from forgiveness now.

Is there anything else you would add to this list?

4. Wherever you are on this journey, it's important to recognize and acknowledge that place. Indicate where you are on the diagram below:

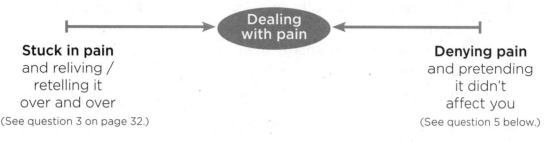

Stuck in pain
and reliving /
retelling it
over and over
(See question 3 on page 32.)

Denying pain
and pretending
it didn't
affect you
(See question 5 below.)

5. Please read the book excerpt below and then answer the questions that follow.

> "Sometimes it seems easier to deny my pain than to do the hard work to deal with and heal what's really there." (*Forgiving What You Can't Forget*, page 21)

How does this resonate with you?

Do you tend to process life through the way you want it to be or the way it actually is?

The more we deny what's going on inside of us, the less likely we'll be to even pull up a seat to the table to process our pain. Read through the list below. Check any statement that comes the closest to something you would say to gloss over your pain:

1. ___ I'm good. I'm fine. I've just decided to move on.
2. ___ It's their loss for walking away from me.
3. ___ God will eventually make everything all right.
4. ___ As a Christian, I know I should forgive, so I have.

5. ___ What's in the past is in the past. I'm just walking forward. No big deal.

6. ___ There's so much to be thankful for, so I'm just choosing to be grateful.

7. ___ Who has the time or energy to unpack why this happened and how it affected me? Let's just move on.

8. ___ I'm mature enough to say, "It is what it is," and get over it.

Take some time now or over the next few days to ask the Lord to help you press past your places of denial. He isn't disappointed or overwhelmed by our level of need. You can journal here or in a separate notebook. Psalm 86:1–7 is a great passage of Scripture to use as you confess your need for healing and help. Also, prayerfully consider reaching out to a trusted friend or seeking the help of a Christian counselor as you begin addressing wounds you've long denied were there.

6. Please read the book excerpt below and then answer the questions that follow.

"When this world—so saturated with flesh resenting flesh, hearts hating hearts, fists slamming fists, pride rising against pride—suddenly sees someone dropping their sword and daring to whisper, 'I forgive' . . . IT STOPS ALL.

In the split second of that utterance, evil is arrested, heaven touches earth, and the richest evidence of the truth of the gospel reverberates not just that day but for generations to come. While salvation is what brings the flesh of a human into perfect alignment with the Spirit of God, forgiveness is the greatest evidence that the Truth of God lives in us." (*Forgiving What You Can't Forget*, page 24)

By what power does this excerpt say we're able to override the resistance of our flesh and the pull of unforgiveness? (See Acts 1:8; Acts 2; and 1 John 4:4 for more study.)

7. When living out God's commands feels too hard, we may need to rewrite the script playing in our heads using Scripture. Highlight the declaration you most need below and then spend some time meditating on the passage of Scripture that goes along with it.

   Are there any other verses that are encouraging you right now? Fill in the the last two rows on page 36 using those passages as a guide to write your own declarations.

MY CURRENT SCRIPT	SCRIPTURE I CAN TURN TO	MY NEW DECLARATION
Living this call of forgiveness is too hard in today's world and in my circumstances.	2 PETER 1:3-4	God has given me everything I need to live for Him through His Word, by His power and in my growing knowledge of His Son Jesus Christ.
My heart is so devastated, I don't have the strength to pray.	ROMANS 8:26-27	It's okay if all I can bring is tears today. The Holy Spirit is interceding for me.
I'm just too broken to have the strength to face any of this.	2 CORINTHIANS 12:9-10	God's grace is sufficient for me. And He is my strength when I don't feel like I can go on.
Honestly, I don't even want to forgive.	PHILIPPIANS 2:13	God is able to give me the power and the desire to do what pleases Him.

MY CURRENT SCRIPT	SCRIPTURE I CAN TURN TO	MY NEW DECLARATION

8. How has forgiveness felt like a "misery" to you in the past? How can you now see forgiveness as a "life-giving freedom"?

God is okay with us asking Him to help our unbelief. Use the space below to write out your own "help my unbelief" prayer.

REVIEW AND READ

Use this time to go back and complete any of the study and reflection questions from previous days this week that you weren't able to finish. Make note of any revelations you've had and reflect on any growth or personal insights you've gained.

Spend the next two days reading chapters 3 and 4 of *Forgiving What You Can't Forget.* Use the space below to make note of anything in the chapters that stands out to you or encourages your heart.

Schedule

WEEK 2

BEFORE GROUP MEETING	Read Chapters 3–4 *Forgiving What You Can't Forget* Book
GROUP MEETING	View Video Session 2: Your Mind, Your Mouth, Your Master Group Discussion Pages 40–45
PERSONAL STUDY DAY 1	Pages 46–51
PERSONAL STUDY DAY 2	Pages 52–57
PERSONAL STUDY DAY 3	Pages 58–63
DAYS 4 & 5 BEFORE WEEK 3 GROUP MEETING	Read Chapters 5–7 *Forgiving What You Can't Forget* Book Complete Any Unfinished Personal Study Activities

YOUR MIND,
YOUR
MOUTH,
YOUR

Master

SESSION 2

WELCOME AND OPENING REFLECTION:

(SUGGESTED TIME: 15–20 MINUTES)

Welcome to session 2 of *Forgiving What You Can't Forget*.

Leader Note: Have a few people share their response to this question before starting the video:

What was your most helpful takeaway from this week's homework?

VIDEO (21:30 MINUTES)

Leader Note: Play the video segment for Session 2.

> ## THIS WEEK'S STATEMENT TO HOLD ONTO:
>
> The best time to forgive is before we're ever offended. The next best time is now.

VIDEO NOTES

Use the outline below to help you follow along with the teaching video or to take additional notes on anything that stands out.

Forgiveness should be one of the first steps, not the last.

"Whatever my feelings will not yet allow for, the blood of Jesus will surely cover."

Forgiveness is both a decision and a process.

The slow unfolding of triggers is actually an act of great mercy from God.

Ephesians 4:26, 29: "In *your* anger do not sin" (v. 26)

What our mind is focused on and what our mouth speaks reveals who we are mastered by.

Pattern we see in Ephesians 4 and throughout Scripture:

1. Warnings not to slander
2. Instructions to be humble
3. Resist the devil

1 Peter 5:6–9: ". . . Your enemy the devil prowls around like a roaring lion . . . resist him . . ." (vv. 8, 9)

James 4:7–8, 10–11: ". . . Resist the devil, and he will flee from you ... Humble yourself before the Lord . . ." (vv. 7, 10)

It's not wrong for us to feel strong emotions, but we must not let our emotions drive us to sin.

Where it may feel too hard to have compassion on the person who has hurt us, we can have compassion on the hurt they must have suffered.

Forgiveness is what brings the flesh of a human into perfect alignment with the Spirit of God.

Matthew 16:24: "Take up your cross and follow me." (NLT)

Luke 23:34: "Father, forgive them, for they know not what they do."

Group DISCUSSION

(*Suggested time:* 40–45 minutes)

Leader Note: We have suggested questions to start with, but feel free to pick any of the additional questions as well. Consider the timeframe of your group and know the ultimate goal is meaningful discussion.

SUGGESTED QUESTIONS

1. What is your initial reaction to the idea that forgiveness should be one of the *first* steps in our healing process and not the *last*? What are some of the things we may believe should have to happen *before* we forgive?

2. How have you typically looked at forgiveness—as something that happens as a one-time act or something that happens over time? What kind of freedom can we find in the knowledge that forgiveness is both a decision *and* a process?

3. The deep pain of old hurts getting triggered again and again can feel both frustrating and unfair. But we learned today that the slow unfolding of triggers is actually an act of great mercy from God. How could this slow revealing and healing process—one where God helps us both recognize and address our pain over time—actually be merciful?

4. Have someone read Ephesians 4:26–27 aloud: "'In your anger do not sin': Do not let the sun go down while you are still angry, and do not give the devil a foothold." What would it look like to "weaponize" this verse? How have you personally applied this verse in your own life? How do you feel now that you know it is talking about addressing and processing with God your *own* anger?

5. Today we were reminded through several passages of Scripture that God calls us to live with humble hearts. (See Ephesians 4:29–32; 1 Peter 5:6–9; James 4:7–8, 10–11.) Why do you think humility is so important in the process of forgiveness?

ADDITIONAL QUESTIONS (as time allows)

6. Both in this week's and last week's video, we learned that we must rule over sin with our minds and our mouths. What are some practical ways we can rule over sin with our thoughts? What about with our words? Look at 2 Corinthians 10:3–5 and Romans 12:2 together as a group. How do each of the two passages of Scripture below speak into this?

7. Hurt people hurt people. How can acknowledging the hurt others have suffered help us be more compassionate?

8. Have someone read Lamentations 3:22–23 aloud. How does remembering God's compassion toward us help us live compassionately toward others?

9. Have someone read Matthew 16:24 aloud. In what ways is forgivenes[s] act of denying yourself? What are some of the "rights" we may have [to] lay down in order to offer forgiveness?

CLOSING (SUGGESTED TIME: 5-MINUTES)

Leader Note: End your session by reading the "Between-Sessions Personal Studies" instructions to the group and making sure there are no questions pertaining to the homework. Then take a few minutes to pray over your group, either reading the provided prayer aloud over them or praying your own prayer.

BETWEEN-SESSIONS PERSONAL STUDIES

Every session in the *Forgiving What You Can't Forget Study Guide* includes five days of personal study to help you make meaningful connections between your life and what you're learning each week. This week, you'll work with the material in chapters 3–4 of the book *Forgiving What You Can't Forget.* You'll also have time to read chapters 5–7 of the book in preparation for your next group meeting.

PRAYER

Father God, we confess there are places we've been putting off forgiving. It has felt too hard, too unfair, too soon for these still-raw wounds. But when You ask us to forgive others as Jesus has forgiven us, You aren't being insensitive to our pain. You are graciously showing us how to get free from all of this hurt. You are helping us to become vessels that pour out grace and kindness instead of words and actions we can never take back. Thank You for not asking us to do this on our own. Thank You that Jesus went first, even in this. Help us to look to Him, learn from Him, and follow His lead. We want the peace and wholeness and hope You're offering us through Him. In Jesus' name, amen.

Personal STUDY

DAY 1

STUDY AND REFLECT

Today we're going to spend a little more time reflecting on this week's video and taking a closer look at what's going on inside our minds.

Feeling mentally stuck in our places of woundedness is such a maddening place to be. That place where we just can't seem to stop going back over all the details. The careless words he said. The unbelievable things she did. The callous and caustic ways they treated us in the midst of our pain. And our enemy, Satan, would love for us to set up camp and dwell in these torturous mental spaces. He wants us to believe the lie that we have no control over our thoughts and that it doesn't even matter what we think anyway.

He's a liar, friend.

How we think becomes how we live. And as we learned in this week's video, what consumes us controls us. This means we are going to have to choose: do we want to be ruled by the pain of our past and the people who have hurt us? Or do we want to surrender all control to the God of all peace and comfort? The God of hope and abundant life?

Remember, what our minds are focused on and what our mouths speak reveal who we are mastered by. That's why we're using this first day to address our thoughts. Not to make us feel condemned for our current thought patterns, but so that we can begin to find healing as we establish new ones.

1. Take a few moments to reflect on some of the things you're struggling to forgive. Which situation or occurrence would you say consumes the most of your thought life right now? Write it in the space below.

How much time would you say you spend thinking about this situation?

——1——2——3——4——5——6——7——8——9——10——

I think about
it in passing
occasionally.

Most days
hold thoughts
about it.

I am struggling to
function at all. I just
can't stop thinking
about it.

How do those thoughts typically leave you feeling? (Examples: enraged, exhausted, irritated, sad, overwhelmed, out of control, hurt, broken, etc.)

2. Scripture has a lot to say about what we meditate on. This is because what feeds us affects us. And what we're thinking on is actually what our mind is feasting on.

Let's look to God's Word for wisdom. Use the lines provided after each verse to write out what we're being encouraged to fix our thoughts on. You'll also find a space to write what is openly stated or implied that we *not* dwell on.

Isaiah 26:3: "You keep him in perfect peace
whose mind is stayed on you,
because he trusts in you." (ESV)

Think on this: _____
Not this: _____

Romans 8:5–6: "Those who live according to the flesh have their minds set on what the flesh desires; but those who live in accordance with the Spirit have their minds set on what the Spirit desires. The mind governed by the flesh is death, but the mind governed by the Spirit is life and peace." (NLT)

Think on this: _____

Not this: _____

Philippians 4:6–8: "Do not be anxious about anything, but in every situation, by prayer and petition, with thanksgiving, present your requests to God. And the peace of God, which transcends all understanding, will guard your hearts and your minds in Christ Jesus. Finally, brothers and sisters, whatever is true, whatever is noble, whatever is right, whatever is pure, whatever is lovely, whatever is admirable—if anything is excellent or praiseworthy—think about such things."

Think on this: _____

Not this: _____

When it comes to your thoughts, which passage of Scripture just noted did you most need to be reminded of?

What is the main benefit we find in these verses that comes from prayerfully and faithfully focusing on the Lord and His ways?

How would you describe your own current level of internal peace? Looking back at the verses we just read, what is one step you could take today to increase your peace?

3. Two words that are often connected in discussions on thoughts are *meditate* and *ruminate*. To meditate means to "to focus one's thoughts on: reflect on or ponder over,"[4] while ruminate is a word that means: "to go over in the mind repeatedly and often casually or slowly; or to chew repeatedly for an extended period."[5]

Much like cows chewing on cud, we mentally "chew" on specific thoughts. But we have a choice every moment of every day about what we're going to ruminate on. Will we keep replaying and reliving those old hurts? Or will we purposefully shift our focus and meditate on God's Word, ingesting and digesting the truths we find there?

Open up your Bible and read Psalm 1:1–3 to find out why this matters.

What does this passage of Scripture list as the benefits of keeping God's Word on repeat in our minds?

Is there anyone in your life you can tell lives with God's Word as their delight and their guide? How would you describe them?

How would you describe a person who spends all of their time nursing and rehearsing old wounds? If you've ever known anyone stuck in the pain of their past, what is it like to be around them?

Knowing there is no condemnation, how do you think people would describe being around you? Would you say your thought life is having a positive or a negative impact on you and those you interact with? (If you feel discouraged by your answer, please know that is why we're working on this together. It's also why we'll be inviting Jesus into all of this today.)

4. Read Hebrews 12:1–2. Why do you think it's *particularly* important to "fix our eyes on Jesus" when it comes to this journey of forgiveness?

5. Read the description of Jesus in Hebrews 4:15–16: "For we do not have a high priest who is unable to empathize with our weaknesses, but we have one who has been tempted in every way, just as we are—yet he did not sin. Let us then approach God's throne of grace with confidence, so that we may receive mercy and find grace to help us in our time of need." Romans 8:1 tells us that we can approach the throne of grace with confidence because there is "no condemnation for those who are in Christ Jesus."

When you find yourself resistant to the idea of forgiveness, is your first reaction to turn *toward* Jesus for help or to pull away from Him? If you pull back, what thoughts and feelings do you think motivate that choice—shame, fear, resentment over being asked to forgive?

What does Hebrews 4:15–16 say Jesus offers us freely when we feel weak and incapable? How could these gifts from Him help you in your current struggles with forgiveness?

6. Second Corinthians 10:4–5 reminds us, "The weapons we fight with are not the weapons of the world. On the contrary, they have divine power to demolish strongholds. We demolish arguments and every pretension that sets itself up against the knowledge of God, and we take captive every thought to make it obedient to Christ."

What are some of the most persistent and troubling thought patterns you've been struggling to break free from?

Look back at the above passage. As my friend Wendy Blight says, a stronghold is any deeply rooted sin in your life that prevents you from growing in your relationship with God.[6] This means any actions that are opposed to the truth of the gospel. The longer these actions go unattended they become a fortress that surrounds and imprisons us. Is tearing down strongholds something we can do in our own power? What kind of power does it take?

7. How might we combine the hope we found in Hebrews 4:15–16 about being able to go to Jesus in our weakness with our need for help in our thought life?

End today by writing out a prayer asking Jesus for any specific help you may need with your journey.

DAY 2
STUDY AND REFLECT

Today we're going to reflect on chapter 3 of the book *Forgiving What You Can't Forget.* If you haven't already read chapter 3, please do so before you begin.

1. Please read the book excerpt below and then answer the questions that follow.

> ". . . part of my story is a severely busted-up marriage. The wounds are healing, but there are areas inside of me that are still so raw, so full of freshly exposed nerves, that even the slightest touch can make me react and recoil.
>
> Like a tooth that's been broken enough to expose the nerves, even breathing hurts. Cold liquid that used to be refreshing stabs. Chewing, absolutely not possible. And I'm constantly aware of the possibility of intense pain if I don't protect myself. But, inevitably, I'll forget. And in an unguarded moment, I'll pay for letting down my defenses.
>
> Raw nerves are complicated with teeth and souls, and near to impossible to protect at all times.
>
> So, when I got triggered and some raw, unresolved pain got poked, a venomous string of words shot out of my mouth. And in less time than it takes to snap my fingers, I was undone. Unwell. Unraveled. All the 'progress' I thought I'd made seemed like such a sham." (*Forgiving What You Can't Forget*, page 26)

Describe a time when you were completely caught off guard by triggered emotions:

How did your reaction to that trigger leave you feeling about your ability to forgive, to heal, to move on? Explain below:

2. Please read the book excerpt below and then answer the questions that follow.

> ". . . if healing hasn't been worked out and forgiveness hasn't been walked out, chaos is what will continue to play out." (*Forgiving What You Can't Forget*, page 29)

How might unhealed hurts be playing out in your life right now? Check all that apply.

_____ Chaotic emotions: screaming, yelling, slamming things, uncontrollable crying episodes

_____ Controlling behaviors: silent treatment, pouting, manipulation, sarcasm

_____ Numbing choices: binging on food or television, mindless social media scrolling, excessive spending or drinking

_____ Uncharacteristic choices: breaking personal boundary lines you would normally keep, compromising your integrity in ways you deep down know are dangerous or not morally in line with your beliefs

_____ Other: _____

3. Please read the book excerpt below and then answer the questions that follow.

> "Once pain has been inflicted, it's impossible to remain unaffected. As I said before, the more our pain consumes us, the more it will control us. That person or people who hurt you, who hurt me—they've caused enough pain. There's been enough damage done. So, what do I do with my pain? Acknowledge it. And what do I need to do with the feelings resulting from the pain? Own them as mine to control. Yes, the hurt was caused by someone else, but the resulting feelings are mine to manage.
>
> And I can't manage feelings I don't own."
> (*Forgiving What You Can't Forget*, page 30)

While we don't want to continually dwell on our pain and get stuck there, we do need to fully address it. David is someone in Scripture who provides a beautiful example of acknowledging all of his feelings. Throughout the Psalms, we find David pouring out all of his hurts, fears, and frustrations before the Lord. Read Psalm 13:1–6 and Psalm 38:8–15 in your Bible. Pay close attention to any verses where you find David expressing his gut-honest emotions instead of stuffing or numbing those emotions.

Did David use any words that currently describe how you feel? List them below.

Have you ever felt shocked or surprised by David's level of honesty in Scripture? Why or why not? How do you think the Lord felt about David's candor, considering the fact David's words are included in Scripture?

How does David's honesty in prayer resemble Art's process of "boxing it out with the Lord" that we learned about in this week's video?

4. Look back at Hebrews 4:15–16 either in your Bible or where we studied it in question 5 yesterday. When the author of this passage of Scripture says we can approach the throne of God with "confidence," the Greek word used is **parrhēsía**. It is a word that means "all out-spokenness, i.e. frankness, bluntness, publicity; by implication, assurance."[7]

What if you allowed yourself to be as honest with the Lord as David was? What feelings do you need to own so God can help you start managing them and healing them?

Take a few minutes and imagine yourself writing out your own psalm in the midst of your pain. Jot down your unfiltered thoughts and emotions in the space below or in a separate journal. Remember: God doesn't pull away from our honesty; it's what He wants from us.

> "The LORD is near to all who call on him,
>   to all who call on him in truth." **Psalm 145:18**

5. Please read the book excerpt below and then answer the questions that follow.

"What we look for is what we will see. What we see determines our perspective. And our perspective becomes our reality. I want my reality to stop being defined by the hopeless pursuit of rewriting yesterday. I want to accept what happened—without letting it steal all my future possibilities—and learn to move on.

Remember those markings of time? BC: Before Crisis. AD: After Devastation. Well, there's a third line I've discovered. It's RH: Resurrected Hope.

Honestly, I wish that's the way the history of time would be marked. After all, that's such a truer reflection of where we are all living. Not 2020 after Christ's death. The reality is that Jesus' death only lasted three days, but His resurrected hope has carried us into the future.

The possibility of hope is what I want to look for so that hope is what I will see. And when I start to notice it, that noticing has a multiplying effect." (*Forgiving What You Can't Forget*, page 32)

How much time and mental energy do you spend wishing you could rewrite yesterday? The scale we used on Day 1 of this week may give you some clue if you feel unsure.

What parts of your present or even your future have you labeled with the word *impossible* because of past pain? How might you look at your future differently if you used the lens of resurrection?

6. When we feel as if there's no hope of ever moving on, we must confront that lie and replace it with the truth of God's Word. Our hope cannot be tied to what people do or do not do. Our hope is tied to a God of *possibility*. Fill in the passages of Scripture below using the NIV translation. Circle the one that brings you the most comfort today.

> "_____ the former things;
>> do not _____ on the past.
> See, I am doing a _____ thing!
>> Now it springs up; do you not perceive it?
> I am making a way in the _____
>> and streams in the _____." Isaiah 43:18–19

"Jesus looked at them and said, 'With man this is _____, but with God _____ things are _____.'" Matthew 19:26

"Ah, Sovereign Lord, you have made the heavens and the earth by your great _____ and outstretched arm. _____ is too hard for you." Jeremiah 32:17

7. Just as David ended his psalms with his eyes on the Lord for hope, that is what we're going to do today too. We don't have to let the hurts

inflicted by others hold us hostage another day longer. Take some time to prayerfully fill in this personalized version of the declaration found on page 32 of *Forgiving What You Can't Forget.* You can also do this in a separate journal if you have several people you need to release.

Today is the day it stops. Today is my day to stop the grim, hopeless pursuit of expecting _____ *to make this right. I release them from having to come back and* _____ *in order for me to heal. You are my Healer, Lord. You are my Restorer. And I'm placing my hope and trust in You so that I can receive the glorious hope-filled possibilities of this new day.*

FIGURING OUT FORGIVENESS

How do we become more like Jesus? We know the basics will involve things like reading our Bible and praying. But Scripture points out another integral part of this process—we join in the suffering that Jesus endured. As we endure suffering and tribulation, God uses it to transform us into the image of Christ. (See Colossians 1:24, 1 Peter 4:1–2, 1 Peter 5:1.)

So instead of giving into the mindset that we can't forgive like Jesus because we're not Jesus, we can know this process of forgiving is actually *shaping* us to be more and more like Jesus. What a beautiful truth. The more we cooperate with forgiveness, the more we're being conformed into the image of God's Son. Will it be painful at times to work with Him in this way? Yes. But is God able to use all of this for good? He truly is.

"And we know that in all things God works for the good of those who love him, who have been called according to his purpose. For those God foreknew he also predestined to be conformed to the image of his Son, that he might be the firstborn among many brothers and sisters." Romans 8:28–29

DAY 3
STUDY AND REFLECT

Today we're going to reflect on chapter 4 of the book *Forgiving What You Can't Forget.* If you haven't already read chapter 4, please do so before you begin.

1. Please read the book excerpt below and then answer the questions that follow.

> "'For me to move forward, for me to see beyond this current darkness, is between me and the Lord. I don't need to wait on others to do anything or wait for blame or shame that won't do anyone any good. I simply must obey whatever God is asking of me right now. God has given me a new way to walk. And God has given me a new way to see. It's forgiveness. And it is beautiful.'
>
> I have to place my healing in the Lord's hands. I need to focus on what I can do to step toward Him in obedience. And forgiveness is what He's asking of me.
>
> I must separate my healing from others' repentance or lack thereof. My ability to heal cannot be conditional on them wanting my forgiveness but only on my willingness to give it.
>
> And I have to separate my healing from any of this being fair. My ability to heal cannot be conditional on the other person receiving adequate consequences for their disobedience but only on my obedience to trust God's justice whether I ever see it or not.
>
> My healing is my choice.
>
> I can heal. I can forgive. I can trust God. And none of those beautiful realities are held hostage by another person."
> (*Forgiving What You Can't Forget*, pages 40–41)

In chapter 4 of *Forgiving What You Can't Forget*, we got to read about two healing miracles that didn't involve anyone but Jesus and the ones who needed healing. (See John 5:1–15; John 9.) Which of these stories did you resonate with the most? Why?

What is your initial reaction to the idea that your ability to heal cannot depend on anyone's choices but your own?

2. Open up your Bible to John 5, the location of the story about the lame man Jesus healed. Write out the question we find Jesus asking this man in verse 6: _____

This is the question He is asking us, precious friend. Do we want to be made well? Because if we do, there are some things we are going to have to lay down. Look back at the text from the book in question 1. Is there anything you still need to lay down that's keeping you from healing? Write all of those things below.

3. Please read the book excerpt below and then answer the questions that follow.

> "Hurt feelings sometimes don't want to cooperate with holy instructions. That's why I have to add some of what Jesus did on the cross into this process. The cross was the most holy act of forgiveness that ever took place. And it was His blood shed for our sins that was the redemptive ingredient that accomplished a forgiveness we could never have obtained or earned for ourselves. . . .

It only makes sense that I include Jesus' shed blood into my act of forgiveness when accomplishing it on my own feels so hard . . . maybe even impossible. Jesus makes it possible."
(*Forgiving What You Can't Forget*, pages 43–44)

We're going to walk through the forgiveness exercise taught by counselor Jim Cress at the end of Day 3, but it's important for us to understand why the blood of Jesus matters in this process. Especially when it comes to the last step. Let's take the time to dig into some verses in Scripture that talk about the importance of the imagery of blood here.

First, read Hebrews 9:22. What did God establish as a requirement for the forgiveness of sin in Old Testament law?

Look up Leviticus 1:4–5; 17:11. Where did the priests in the Old Testament get the blood from in order to provide an offering for the atonement of sin?

Now look up Hebrews 9:11–14. What did Jesus, our High Priest, offer up "once for all" as the final and ultimate sacrifice?

How does it make you feel to know that Jesus shed His blood for you? How does it impact you to think that He was willing to pour out His blood for the forgiveness of every person who has ever hurt you?

4. Not only does Jesus offer us full forgiveness through the shedding of His blood, it's important for us to take note of *when* He offered that forgiveness. Read the verses below and then answer a few questions:

"When they came to the place called the Skull, they crucified him there, along with the criminals—one on his right, the other on his left. Jesus said, 'Father, forgive them, for they do not know what they are doing.' And they divided up his clothes by casting lots." Luke 23:33-34

"But God demonstrates his own love for us in this: While we were still sinners, Christ died for us." Romans 5:8

When did Jesus' offering of forgiveness occur—before or after forgiveness was asked for by those who had sinned against Him? Before or after anyone had owned or admitted they had done anything wrong?

What does this speak to your heart about when we should offer forgiveness to others?

5. Please read the book excerpt below and then do the exercise that follows.

"For now, I realize the hurt that passed through them to me is a more epic moment of opportunity than I ever realized. That hurt can either pass through me and be unleashed on others. Or, it can be stopped by me, right here, right now. The world can become a little darker or a little brighter just by the choice I make in this moment." (*Forgiving What You Can't Forget*, page 53)

This is our moment to stop playing a part in these relentless cycles of hurt. Remember, all we need to bring is our willingness, not the fullness of our restored feelings.

We learned this week that forgiveness is both a decision and a process. We must first forgive for the facts of what happened in a marked moment of forgiveness. Then when we are triggered with lingering pain or hard memories after our decision to forgive, we have an opportunity to continue the process of forgiveness by forgiving the impact that their actions are still having on us.

The forgiveness exercise discussed in this chapter can be a tremendous help in this process. **That's why we have provided the cards you will need in the back of this study guide.** You can tear them out and use the directions below to help you walk through this exercise. Please don't feel the pressure to do this activity all at once.

THE FORGIVENESS EXERCISE

● Fill out each white card provided with this information:

Person: The name of the person who hurt you.
Fact: This is what happened and what I need to forgive.
Impact: This is how this still affects me—how I get triggered and my pain feels fresh all over again.

● Now turn over your card and fill out I forgive _____ for _____.

● Place the cards on the table or floor.

● Declare your forgiveness by placing the red cards provided over each white card.

● As you do so, say, "I forgive _____ for _____. And whatever my feelings won't yet allow for, the blood of Jesus will surely cover."

● Repeat this exercise until you are done interacting with each card.

● Know that you can walk out this process in your mind even when you do not have these cards readily available.

You are doing such incredible work, friend. When it feels too hard, know that you aren't walking through any of this alone. The Lord will never leave you or forsake you, even in the messiest and hardest moments of the journey. He is with you on the days you feel like you're making good progress. He is with you on the days you just want to throw this study guide across the room and be done with it all. He is with you. And He loves you without end.

DAYS 4 & 5
REVIEW AND READ

Use this time to go back and complete any of the study and reflection questions from previous days this week that you weren't able to finish. Make note of any revelations you've had and reflect on any growth or personal insights you've gained.

Spend the next two days reading chapters 5–7 of *Forgiving What You Can't Forget.* Use the space below to make note of anything in the chapters that stands out to you or encourages your heart.

Schedule

WEEK 3

BEFORE GROUP MEETING	Read Chapters 5-7 *Forgiving What You Can't Forget* Book
GROUP MEETING	View Video Session 3: The Divine Echo Group Discussion Pages 66-71
PERSONAL STUDY DAY 1	Pages 72-77
PERSONAL STUDY DAY 2	Pages 77-83
PERSONAL STUDY DAY 3	Pages 83-88
DAYS 4 & 5 BEFORE WEEK 2 GROUP MEETING	Read Chapters 8-9 *Forgiving What You Can't Forget* Book Complete Any Unfinished Personal Study Activities

THE
DIVINE

SESSION 3

WELCOME AND OPENING REFLECTION:

(SUGGESTED TIME: 15–20 MINUTES)

Welcome to session 3 of *Forgiving What You Can't Forget*.

Leader Note: Have a few people share their response to this question before starting the video:

What was your most helpful takeaway from this week's homework?

VIDEO (27:00 MINUTES)

Leader Note: Play the video segment for session 3.

> ## THIS WEEK'S STATEMENT TO HOLD ONTO:
>
> We can't change what we have experienced, but we can choose how the experiences change us.

VIDEO NOTES

Use the outline below to help you follow along with the teaching video or to take additional notes on anything that stands out.

Our perceptions can skew the way we view reality. And if we live with a skewed reality, we can't heal completely.

Just because we think something is true doesn't make it true.

Adam and Eve:

- Chosen by God
- Breathed on and touched by God
- The only part of creation made in the image of God

The Hebrew word for *suitable* is **neged,** meaning "what is in front of you, in your sight, before your face, in your view."[8]

Genesis 1:28, "God blessed them and said to them, 'Be fruitful and increase in number, fill the earth, and subdue it . . .'"

The Divine Echo = As image bearers we are to fill the earth with evidence of the goodness of God and the glory of God. And the more we remind each other of who we really are, the more God's goodness and glory echo throughout the earth.

Isaiah 14:13–14: ". . . I will make myself like the Most High."

Ezekiel 28:17–19: The fall of Lucifer

Genesis 2:25: Adam and Eve stand naked and unashamed.

Genesis 1:31: "God saw all that he had made, and it was very good."

Psalm 4:2: "How long will you people turn my glory into shame?"

Seeing others as made in the image of God isn't based on their choices . . . it's based on God's truth.

We don't need to wait for other people to do right things before we make right choices that honor God.

You are more than what's happened to you. You are made in the holy image of God, designed by God, loved by God.

God is in charge of the fixing. And that frees us to just do the living and the loving together.

Group DISCUSSION

(Suggested time: 40–45 minutes)

Leader Note: We have suggested questions to start with, but feel free to pick any of the additional questions as well. Consider the timeframe of your group and know the ultimate goal is meaningful discussion.

SUGGESTED QUESTIONS

1. Just because we think something is true doesn't make it true. What are some possible examples of skewed perceptions that could lead to our inability to completely heal from past hurts?

2. We learned today that Adam needed a visual—something in front of him to view. Eve, in being a helper suitable for him, was to be a reminder of who he was ... a reflection of the glory of God and goodness of God. Why is echoing this truth back and forth to each other so vital? What are some practical ways we can do this?

3. Have someone read Genesis 1:26–28 aloud. Do you typically view people as made in the image of God only if they make godly choices? How might this idea of honoring others as being made in the image of God and loved

by God, no matter what they have done, change the way we interact with them?

4. One of the things we learned today is that God is in charge of the fixing. This doesn't mean we aren't to address needed changes. We just aren't supposed to put the responsibility of changing them on ourselves. Do you live more like it's God's job to change people or yours? How can you practically live this out in some of your current relationships?

5. Turn to Ephesians 6:12 and have someone read it aloud. When we are deeply hurt, it's easy to label the person who has hurt us as the enemy. Who does this verse say is our real enemy? Why is it so important to keep this in mind during the process of forgiveness?

ADDITIONAL QUESTIONS (as time allows)

6. Continuing to think about Ephesians 6:12, what are some of the most effective weapons we can choose to use in this spiritual battle we're facing?

7. The anthem of shame is this: "You are what you've done. The worst of what others say about you is true. What you did is all you'll ever be." Why do you think Satan loves it when we define ourselves by what we've done or what's been done to us? Why does he want us to get stuck in a place of defining other people by what they've done?

8. Have someone read Philippians 1:6 to the group. How can this verse h...
us release control of trying to change other people?

CLOSING (SUGGESTED TIME: 5-MINUTES)

Leader Note: End your session by reading the "Between-Sessions Personal Studies" instructions to the group and making sure there are no questions pertaining to the homework. Then take a few minutes to pray over your group, either reading the provided prayer aloud over them or praying your own prayer.

BETWEEN-SESSIONS PERSONAL STUDIES

Every session in the *Forgiving What You Can't Forget Study Guide* includes five days of personal study to help you make meaningful connections between your life and what you're learning each week. This week, you'll work with the material in chapters 5–7 of the book *Forgiving What You Can't Forget.* You'll also have time to read chapters 8–9 of the book in preparation for your next group meeting.

PRAYER

Father God, we come to You confessing that we need Your help with our thinking. We want to be women led by wisdom and truth. Women shaped and steadied by wisdom and truth. Women well-equipped to process our pain through wisdom and truth. That's why we're asking You to help us as we head into this new week of studying. Help us to see the truth. About You. About ourselves. About those who have hurt us. And continue to help us to see the truth of our need to forgive and be forgiven. We love You. We need You. And while we want You to move in our circumstances, we realize the most important place we need You to move right now is in the way we think and see. In Jesus' name, amen.

Personal STUDY

DAY 1
STUDY AND REFLECT

Today we're going to reflect on chapter 5 of the book *Forgiving What You Can't Forget.* If you haven't already read chapter 5, please do so before you begin.

This week is going to focus on a lot of looking back so we can move forward. It's a process that may feel messy and hard. It's definitely one we're going to feel tempted to rush through at times. But we must remember . . . quick fixes are never deep fixes. They only interrupt the true process of broken to beautiful.

Restoration is as messy as it is marvelous, and it always takes its sweet time. There aren't straight, short lines from hurt to healing. It's a process that wraps around you, curves into the crevices and recesses where unresolved pain hides, and envelops you deeply and completely. What can feel like a tomb is actually a cocoon where life will one day burst forth and you'll have gained the strength to finally fly.

Let's keep moving toward hope and freedom . . .

1. Please read the book excerpt below and then answer the questions that follow.

    "We all have a story. And then we all have a story we tell ourselves. Revisiting the past can be scary. But if we want to fully heal, we need to dig into our stories to understand what's behind the curtain. Forgiveness isn't just about what's in front of us. Sometimes, a bigger part of the journey is uncovering what is informing us from long ago. Woven throughout our experiences is a connecting thread that pulls the beliefs we formed from our past into the very present moments of today." (*Forgiving What You Can't Forget*, page 57)

    What is your initial reaction to the idea of revisiting your past?

    Did any bits and pieces of your own story start surfacing as you read through chapter 5? Write a few of those below, both the painful and the beautiful.

2. Without going into details or spending too much time, if you had to define some major themes in your life in just a few words, what words would you use?

3. Before we start officially "collecting dots" from our past, let's allow Scripture to speak truth into our hearts about where God is in our story and what He has to say about us. Read Psalm 139:1–18 in your Bible. Now read it again. Slowly. Prayerfully. Write small "Thank You" phrases to God in the space provided, using any verses that stood out to you or deeply encouraged you.

Here are a few examples:

- Thank You, Lord, that even though I felt abandoned by _____, You are always with me.
- Thank You, Lord, that even though I have felt worthless, You say I'm fearfully and wonderfully made.
- Thank You, Lord, that even though I feel like _____ failed to protect me, You hem me in and cover me.

Thank You, Lord, _____

_____.

Thank You, Lord, _____

_____.

Thank You, Lord, _____

_____.

Please read the book excerpt below and then answer the questions that follow.

> "The greatest hell a human can experience here on earth is not suffering. It's feeling like the suffering is pointless and it will never get any better." (*Forgiving What You Can't Forget*, page 66)

4. When in your own life have you felt afraid that your suffering might be endless and pointless? Is it with a hard relationship where your needs went unmet or a mistake you made or a wrong you've suffered and has never been made right? Write anything that comes to mind.

Read the passages of Scripture below and write in your own words what they teach us about suffering.

2 Corinthians 1:3–4:

2 Corinthians 4:17:

James 1:2–4:

1 Peter 5:10:

Revelation 21:4–5:

Have you seen any of these truths already playing out in your own life? Record your thoughts below.

5. We serve a God who is able to turn our pain into purpose. And while Satan wants to use our stories against us, Scripture tells us that we can use our stories as weapons against *him*.

Revelation 12:10–11 reads, ". . . For the accuser of our brothers and sisters, who accuses them before our God day and night, has been hurled down. They triumphed over him by the blood of the Lamb and by the word of their testimony."

Why is sharing our story of God's redemption in our life so important?

How might God want to take the pain in your life and turn it into hope-giving, hell-defeating purpose? Where have you already seen God do that in your life or someone else's?

6. Please read the book excerpt below and then answer the questions that follow.

"My counselor likes to encourage me to collect the dots, connect the dots, and then correct the dots. We'll do the connecting and correcting in future chapters. But right now, at this moment, let's start at the beginning and allow your memories to leak out in liquid pen strokes. Don't fear how the words come out or get tangled up in any sort of timeline, or feel like you have to ensure every detail is precise and correct. It's not about getting it all right but rather getting it all out." (*Forgiving What You Can't Forget*, page 70)

Grab your journal and a pen and prayerfully ask God to help you continue what we started in the very first question today—collecting dots from your own story.

What are some of the words and events that have most deeply shaped and impacted your life? Take the time to write down both the beautiful and the painful memories. Go back as far as you can remember and work your way through your childhood, teen years, young adulthood, all the way up till today. Don't edit or censor yourself. Simply ask God to help write out as much as you can. After writing in your journal, give consideration to any areas of unforgiveness you need to tend to. Make note of that here.

Remember ... this hard work is *holy* work. It's *good* work. And you'll be so thankful you stuck with it to the end. Keep going, beautiful friend.

A NOTE ON JOURNALING

Chapters 5, 6, and 7 of *Forgiving What You Can't Forget* are filled with incredibly beneficial questions to help you with this process of collecting, connecting, and correcting the dots in your life. While we won't be able to go through all of these questions within the time and space constraints of this Bible study, we highly recommend and encourage you to set aside time to work through all of them at your own pace. There is also a unique interactive companion to *Forgiving What You Can't Forget* you can purchase that will help you engage with the specific questions from the chapters on an even deeper personal level. You can purchase *The Forgiveness Journal: A Guided Journey to Forgiving What You Can't Forget* at your favorite retailer.

DAY 2
STUDY AND REFLECT

Today we're going to reflect on chapter 6 of the book *Forgiving What You Can't Forget.* If you haven't already read chapter 6, please do so before you begin.

1. Please read the book excerpt below and then answer the questions that follow.

> "What we experience all throughout life impacts the perceptions we carry. The longer we carry those perceptions, the more they become the truths we believe, live by, operate under, and use to help us navigate life today.

It's important to start making these connections between what happened in our growing-up years and the reasons we do some of the things we do, say some of the things we say, and believe some of the things we believe right now. And it's not just processing for the sake of understanding ourselves better. It's processing what still needs to be forgiven so we can truly move forward in healthy ways. The things marking us from yesterday are still part of the making of us today." (*Forgiving What You Can't Forget*, page 72)

The things that happen in our lives don't just tell a story. They inform us of the story we tell ourselves. Look back at what you journaled about at the end of yesterday and take some time to answer the following questions to help you start connecting some of the dots you've collected.

Record some events from your past that instilled a clear idea of what you believe you should and shouldn't do or that you should be or shouldn't be. These can be experiences you've walked through or perceptions your family passed on to you.

How did some of these events or perceptions impact what you believe about other people?

How have these events or perceptions influenced what you believe about yourself?

How have these events or perceptions affected what you believe about God?

How have these events or perceptions shaped what you believe about things like forgiveness, resentment, retaliation, and reconciliation?

2. Considering your answers, which areas of belief are you already beginning to see will need some correcting?

How might your life be negatively impacted and your healing process be impeded if you don't address these skewed perceptions?

3. Please read the book excerpt below and then answer the questions that follow.

> "It was only when my most honest opinion of myself was also an honoring opinion of myself that I could stand vulnerable before Art without fear. Without walls of pretension. Or curtains that were only opened when we performed. Without little lies to cover things we couldn't bear to be revealed . . . without piercing judgments of each other's frailties.
>
> Art had to believe he was acceptable.
>
> I had to believe I was accepted.
>
> These weren't feelings to find inside our relationship. These were truths to be lived out because God had already helped us believe them as individuals first. Then, in moments of vulnerability, we could simply remind each other what we already knew to be true." (*Forgiving What You Can't Forget*, page 78)

Would you say that your most honest opinions of yourself are honoring or dishonoring? Explain your answer below.

Over the course of your life, when have you looked to other people to carry the burden of making you feel accepted? Who have you wanted to make you feel better about who you are, fix who you are, or complete who you are?

4. One of the most soul-steadying truths we can begin to believe is that we're already accepted. The NKJV translation of Ephesians 3:6 says God "made us accepted in the Beloved." Open your Bible to Ephesians 1:3–12. As you read through this entire passage of Scripture, write down every word or phrase that represents God defining or describing you.

Which truths from this passage do you find most encouraging?

Why is it important for us to view ourselves as already accepted, loved, and freely forgiven?

What would change about how we interact with others if we viewed them as accepted, loved, and worthy of being freely forgiven?

5. Grasping the truth of Genesis 1:27 is also vital as we work to address our skewed perceptions about ourselves and others.

> "So God created mankind in his own image,
>> in the image of God he created them;
>> male and female he created them." **Genesis 1:27**

Just like Adam and Eve, we are image bearers of God. More than dust and bone. More than what we've done.

The *Imago Dei*, the Latin term used for "image of God," is "permanent, unchangeable, and incapable of being lost. It is of the essence of who we are as humans. This status has been graciously and irrevocably given to all human beings, precisely because they are human."[9]

What are your initial thoughts on the fact that this status of being created in the image of God is a gift given and not one we have to attain?

6. Now take a few moments and use the questions below to help you take an honest assessment of how you view the people you've been struggling to forgive. You don't have to start with the one who hurt you the most. But start with someone. You may even want to spend some extra time processing this on a deeper level in your personal journal.

Who in your life do you need to see for who they really are, not just for what they've done?

How can you start viewing them as more than just dust and bone? Where do you see the breath and touch of God in them?

"Then Peter came to Jesus and asked, 'Lord, how many times shall I forgive my brother or sister who sins against me? Up to seven times?' Jesus answered, 'I tell you, not seven times, but seventy-seven times.'" Matthew 18:21–22

We know we aren't to keep a record of wrongs, so surely this verse doesn't mean we should count up how many times we've forgiven someone. So what does it mean?

Leon Morris states in his commentary on the book of Matthew, "This, of course, is not counseling an essay in arithmetic so that the seventy-eighth offense need not be forgiven. It is a way of saying that for Jesus' followers forgiveness is to be unlimited. For them forgiveness is a way of life. Bearing in mind what they have been forgiven, they cannot withhold forgiveness from any who sin against them."[10]

So, Jesus isn't providing us with a certain amount of times to forgive. He's calling us to let it become a perpetual state of being. To live with a forgiveness mindset.

7. We all need grace. We all need forgiveness. We all need compassion and healing. We're also at different points on a journey of sanctification.

Sanctification is the Lord's continual process of making us holy and wholly set apart for Him. While we have been "definitively" sanctified, meaning God sees us as pure and holy through the lens of Jesus and His completed work on the cross, we are still being "progressively" sanctified. That means we are being shaped to be more and more like Christ.

Look up 1 Thessalonians 5:23.

Who is in charge of this sanctifying work?

Is there anyone in your life who you have been trying to "sanctify" or fix yourself? Write out a prayer of release concerning that person as you end today. Ask God to help you surrender complete control of trying to change that person's heart. And ask Him to help you lean into and cooperate with the good work of sanctification He is doing in you even now. God's part is the fixing. Our part is the loving.

DAY 3
STUDY AND REFLECT

Today we're going to reflect on chapter 7 of the book *Forgiving What You Can't Forget.* If you haven't already read chapter 7, please do so before you begin.

1. Please read the book excerpt below and then answer the questions that follow.

> ". . . it's impossible to travel through life and not collect emotional souvenirs. We are either carrying healthy perspectives or files of proof from our past—evidence of what's happened to us and how we've been wronged. Basically, files of proof left unattended turn into grudges and resentments that weigh us down and skew our perspectives. When we choose to walk down the path of correcting the dots, we aren't changing where we've been but we're sorting through our souvenirs to determine what stays with us from here: unhelpful proof or healthier perspectives." (*Forgiving What You Can't Forget*, page 96)

What are some of the reasons we may feel we need to collect proof of the pain others have caused us?

Why might we feel resistant or afraid to let go of our proof?

How have you seen "collecting and keeping proof of how you've been hurt" play out in your own life? Is it something you rarely do or continually do?

2. Let's look at a familiar passage of Scripture in a new light.

> "Love is patient, love is kind. It does not envy, it does not boast, it is not proud. It does not dishonor others, it is not self-seeking, it is not easily angered, it keeps no record of wrongs."
> **1 Corinthians 13:4–5**

It would be easy to read these verses and think that this kind of love mostly benefits the person receiving it. That the recipient of our kindness, our patience, our refusal to keep a record of wrongs is the one getting the greatest good. But what if these verses are also a gift to *us*? Think back to what we've read in chapter 7.

What are some of the ways collecting proof actually does us *harm*?

How might God's reminder that love doesn't keep case files actually be a freeing and kind gift to us?

3. An important reminder we keep coming back to throughout this study is the truth that we all need forgiveness.

Look up these verses and write them out in the space provided.

Romans 3:23:

Psalm 130:3:

Ecclesiastes 7:20:

And yet . . . God, in His great mercy, also offers us these truths:

> "Surely it was for my benefit
>   that I suffered such anguish.
> In your love you kept me
>   from the pit of destruction;
> you have put all my sins
>   behind your back." **Isaiah 38:17**

> "I, even I, am he who blots out
>   your transgressions, for my own sake,
>   and remembers your sins no more." **Isaiah 43:25**

> "When you were dead in your sins and in the uncircumcision of your flesh, God made you alive with Christ. He forgave us all our sins, having canceled the charge of our legal indebtedness, which stood against us and condemned us; he has taken it away, nailing it to the cross. And having disarmed the powers and authorities, he made a public spectacle of them, triumphing over them by the cross." **Colossians 2:13–15**

God has every right to keep a record of all the sins we have committed against Him, but what do these passages of Scripture say He does instead? (See also Isaiah 44:22; Micah 7:18-19.)

Which image in the passages of Scripture we just read means the most to you personally?

What do these verses speak to your heart, considering any detailed lists you've been keeping against others?

"To be forgiven is, as it were, the root; to forgive is the flower." Charles Spurgeon[11]

4. The only things our proof can do is:

- Tell the story of our pain.
- Acknowledge that we don't agree with what happened.
- Help us convince others that what happened wasn't right.

And that's all our proof will ever do.

It can take us to the pain over and over again. But keeping a record of all the wrongs done to us will never be able to take us past the pain. Our proof will never lead us through the pain or let us heal from the pain. The proof only keeps us trapped in the place where the pain occurred so we keep getting hurt over and over again.

This is why we must sit with these questions today. Write out your sincere thoughts below each one.

What do I want most, to be right or to be healed?

Am I ready to do whatever God asks of me so that I can be truly whole and free?

5. Let's look at one more verse where God reminds us that He isn't keeping score when it comes to our sin.

> "Therefore, if anyone is in Christ, the new creation has come: The old has gone, the new is here! All this is from God, who reconciled us to himself through Christ and gave us the ministry of reconciliation: that God was reconciling the world to himself in Christ, not counting people's sins against them. And he has committed to us the message of reconciliation." **2 Corinthians 5:17–19**

What hope! Not only is He a God who freely and fully forgives, He is able to make all things new. He can give us a new way of thinking. A new way of living. A new way of processing our pain.

Even if the other person never changes, even if they never say they're sorry or make things right, we can put off our old ways of thinking and collecting proof and walk in the newness we have in Christ.

What old patterns of thinking and reacting do you personally need to ask God to help you correct? (See also Ephesians 4:22–24, 29–32.)

What new attitudes are you choosing to believe He *can* help you begin walking in?

As you continue working your way through the journaling questions found in chapters 5, 6, and 7 of *Forgiving What You Can't Forget* on your own, stop and let these words become your declaration as you read them out loud today:

"***There is a healed version of me that is waiting and wanting to emerge.*** I am capable of letting go of my proof. Proof only keeps me trapped in the place where the pain occurred, so I keep getting hurt over and over again. I will reject the seduction of nursing my grudges, and I will stop assuming God didn't intervene to help me. Instead of running away I will run to God when I need help. Perspective is what I'm holding on to and what I'm carrying from here. I have collected the dots. Connected the dots. And corrected the dots. Now I am choosing to believe God's most merciful outcome is the one I'm living. I'm not a victim. I am a healed woman walking in victory."(*Forgiving What You Can't Forget*, page 101)

REVIEW AND READ

Use this time to go back and complete any of the study and reflection questions from previous days this week that you weren't able to finish. Make note of any revelations you've had and reflect on any growth or personal insights you've gained.

Spend the next two days reading chapters 8–9 of *Forgiving What You Can't Forget.* Use the space below to make note of anything in the chapters that stands out to you or encourages your heart.

Schedule

WEEK 4

BEFORE GROUP MEETING	Read Chapters 8–9 *Forgiving What You Can't Forget* Book
GROUP MEETING	View Video Session 4: There's Always a Meanwhile Group Discussion Pages 92–98
PERSONAL STUDY DAY 1	Pages 99–104
PERSONAL STUDY DAY 2	Pages 104–110
PERSONAL STUDY DAY 3	Pages 111–116
DAYS 4 & 5 BEFORE WEEK 3 GROUP MEETING	Read Chapters 10–11 *Forgiving What You Can't Forget* Book Complete Any Unfinished Personal Study Activities

THERE'S ALWAYS A *Meanwhile*

SESSION 4

...COME AND OPENING REFLECTION:
(...GESTED TIME: 15-20 MINUTES)

Welcome to session 4 of *Forgiving What You Can't Forget*.

Leader Note: Have a few people share their response to this question before starting the video:

What was your most helpful takeaway from this week's homework?

VIDEO (24:00 MINUTES)

Leader Note: Play the video segment for Session 4.

> ## THIS WEEK'S STATEMENT TO HOLD ONTO:
> With God, there's always a meanwhile.

VIDEO NOTES

Use the outline below to help you follow along with the teaching video or to take additional notes on anything that stands out.

Genesis 50:20: "You intended to harm me, but God intended it for good to accomplish what is now being done, the saving of many lives."

There's a physical reality we see right in front of us, but there's also a spiritual reality of what our good God is always doing.

Genesis 37:2–4:

- Jacob's family line
- Joseph hated by his brothers

Unattended-to hurt in the human heart can often turn to hate.

Genesis 37:5–11: Joseph's dreams

Genesis 37:12–20: Joseph's brothers plot against him.

Genesis 37:36: *"Meanwhile . . ."*

- Joseph sold to Potiphar

The meanwhile . . . God uses the rejection of Joseph's brothers as a protection of Joseph's calling.

Genesis 39:
- Joseph honors God where he is
- Joseph falsely accused by Potiphar's wife and sent to prison

The meanwhile . . . God actually uses this unfair commotion as a means for Joseph's promotion.

Genesis 40:14–15: Joseph's request of the cupbearer while in prison

Genesis 41:1: Two full years later . . .

Even if we don't know how everything's going to turn out, we can know that the goodness of God will be with us in the hardest moments and the longest days.

Forgiveness is the perfect start to our healing. It shouldn't be our last resort.

Genesis 41:14: Pharaoh sends for Joseph.

When it's the right time, God's time becomes quick time.

Genesis 41:39–40: Joseph goes from prison to the second most powerful man in all the land of Egypt.

We do not serve a do-nothing God.

Group DISCUSSION

(*Suggested time:* 40–45 minutes)

Leader Note: We have suggested questions to start with, but feel free to pick any of the additional questions as well. Consider the timeframe of your group and know the ultimate goal is meaningful discussion.

SUGGESTED QUESTIONS

1. Joseph's life shows us so clearly that we do not serve a do-nothing God, and that with God there's always a meanwhile. What hope can we find in these truths when it specifically comes to the journey of forgiveness?

2. When life feels painful and unfair, we often want God to rescue us right away. Joseph went through *thirteen years* of extreme hardship. How might we be tempted to find this truth discouraging? Knowing that God had purpose tucked into every moment of Joseph's journey, how can we actually let it encourage us when our own story feels unending?

3. The physical reality we see right in front of us is never the full story. Our lives are "both-and" stories—both the pain of our physical reality and the good God is working in the spiritual reality. What might be the danger in assuming that if we can't see God working, He must not be working? How does it encourage you to know our lives are "both-and"?

4. Read 2 Corinthians 4:16–18 out loud. What are some of the ways we often get stuck seeing only our physical realities? How can we sincerely begin living each day with our eyes fixed on what is unseen and eternal?

5. God used rejection for Joseph's protection and all of the unfair commotion for Joseph's promotion. When has God used something that felt detrimental in your life or the life of someone you know to bring about a surprising good?

ADDITIONAL QUESTIONS (as time allows)

6. Taking into account all that Joseph went through, how do you think you would have felt if you had been in his place? What part of his story would you have struggled with the most?

7. Open your Bible to Proverbs 4:23 and have someone read it aloud. Joseph's brothers did not address the hurt in their own hearts. How do their actions prove the importance of Proverbs 4:23? What can we learn from their choices about the need to tend to any hurt, anger, and bitterness in our own hearts?

8. Turn to Psalm 27:13–14 and read it aloud. When we're tempted to focus on the unfairness of our situation, how can we instead choose to look for God's goodness?

CLOSING (SUGGESTED TIME: 5-MINUTES)

Leader Note: End your session by reading the "Between-Sessions Personal Studies" instructions to the group and making sure there are no questions pertaining to the homework. Then take a few minutes to pray over your group, either reading the provided prayer aloud over them or praying your own prayer.

BETWEEN-SESSIONS PERSONAL STUDIES

Every session in the *Forgiving What You Can't Forget Study Guide* includes five days of personal study to help you make meaningful connections between your life and what you're learning each week. This week, you'll work with the material in chapters 8–9 of the book *Forgiving What You Can't Forget.* You'll also have time to read chapters 10–11 of the book in preparation for your next group meeting.

*r God, we are so thankful for the reminder that You are not
...nothing God. You see us. You love us. And You have not
for one second forsaken us. Give us the wisdom we need for the
circumstances we are currently in. Help us to choose faithfulness
and obedience to You, even when we don't understand what
You're doing. We know there isn't a single thing the enemy can
send our way that You can't overcome . . . that You can't redeem
. . . that You can't use for our good and the good of others. So,
we're choosing the way of forgiveness. We're trusting in Your
love. And we're surrendering every heartache and difficult cir-
cumstance into Your loving and mighty hands, believing that with
You there's always a meanwhile. In Jesus' name, amen.*

Personal STUDY

DAY 1
STUDY AND REFLECT

Today we're going to reflect more on the video. This will give us a good framework for digging into chapters 8–9 of the book *Forgiving What You Can't Forget* in the days that follow.

Have you ever found yourself wishing life could be as predictable as a movie? One where you know everything is going to turn out okay in the end and everyone involved is going to live happily ever after. Because then it would all feel a whole lot more survivable.

When we watch a love story, it's a lot easier to get through the angst in the middle when we know the lead characters are going to end up together. It's the same for a nail-biting mystery. We may still jump and cringe a little every now and then when the tension gets high, but ultimately we're okay because we know our favorite character is going to make it to the end.

But we aren't living in a movie. We haven't seen any plot-revealing trailers. We can't go online and read through the spoilers so we aren't caught off guard. We as human beings living in the real world have to process each scene of life as it comes—good or bad. *or have someone close to us*
we are had thing happen to us
that thing that happened to that have affected

So how do we keep going when we're discouraged by the current script our life seems to be following and we're terrified of what might be coming next?

Let's allow the life of Joseph to encourage us a little more.

1. God had given Joseph a dream for his life. And yet, he kept finding himself in devastating circumstances that seemed to be pointing his life in the wrong direction, all at the hands of other people.

   Use the Scripture references to fill in the chart per the example below with the person/people who acted against Joseph and what they chose to do.

SCRIPTURE	WHO	HURTFUL ACTION
Genesis 37:23-24	Joseph's brothers	Stripped him of his robe and threw him in a cistern
Genesis 37:28		Sold him to traders
Genesis 37:36		Sold to 1 of Pharaoh's officers.
Genesis 39:11-18		Put in jail because the officers wife said he tried to rape her... on + on.
Genesis 39:19-20		
Genesis 40:20-23		

when we look at those actions that were done to Joseph by others,

When you look at this chart, who does it look like was determining the course of Joseph's life and deciding his destiny?

In your own life, does it seem like God is in control or other people?

Where do you currently feel like someone else messed up God's plans for you or ruined your chances for a good life, all because of their choices?

✗ While we are impacted emotionally and even physically by others' actions against us, we don't have to fear or worry that their actions can stop the good plans of our mighty and loving God. Look up Genesis 50:20 and write it below. *(later) Joseph said to his brothers* "You intended harm for me, but God intended it all for good. ~~He brought me to this position~~*

How does this verse encourage your heart?

These examples are unchangeable facts that happened and

3. Joseph probably wouldn't have written his story with all of the painful *hers.* ✗ twists and turns it took. And yet, God had purpose in every moment. *he was able to forgive his bro* God ~~was also with Joseph without fail.~~ Underline every time you find this truth in the passage of Scripture below. *✗ Back to p. 110*

> "But while Joseph was there in the prison, the LORD was with him; he showed him kindness and granted him favor in the eyes of the prison warden. So the warden put Joseph in charge of all those held in the prison, and he was made responsible for all that was done there. The warden paid no attention to anything under Joseph's care, because the LORD was with Joseph and gave him success in whatever he did." **Genesis 39:20b–23**

God has also promised to be with us and never forsake us. (See Deuteronomy 31:6; Hebrews 13:5.)

How aware are you of God's continual presence in your life? Is it something you think you have to feel or something you know and believe is a fact?

What are some things you could do this week to help yourself become more aware of Him? (Ideas: Setting an alarm to prompt you several times a day to stop and thank Him for being with you, memorizing Scripture about His presence, etc.)

4. Reading a passage of Scripture in different translations can add richness and depth of understanding. Let's read two different versions of Psalm 32:8 and answer a few questions.

> "The Lord says, 'I will guide you along the best pathway for your life. I will advise you and watch over you.'" (NLT)

> "I will instruct you and teach you in the way you should go; I will counsel you with my loving eye on you." (NIV)

In what ways do you feel as if there is no way the path you are on right now can possibly be God's best pathway for your life?

I hope that

How can Joseph's story and the reminders from Scripture today help you trust that God can bring good, even from all of this?

we know that there are

~~When have the~~ difficult circumstances in your life ~~left you~~ that leave us feeling like God is distant or disinterested?

I hope the story of Joseph is a reminder that us

~~How does it encourage you to know~~ He is watching and guiding you with His "loving eye" on you?

5. "Casting all your cares [all your anxieties, all your worries, and all your concerns, once and for all] on Him, for He cares about you [with deepest affection, and watches over you very carefully]." (1 Peter 5:7 AMP)

   Spend a few minutes meditating on the Scripture above and then answer the questions below: Think about these

   ✓ ● What worries about your future do you need to specifically and fully release to God today?

   _____

   _____

   _____

   ● What fears about the choices of others do you need Him to help you trust He can use for good?

   _____

   _____

   _____

   ✓ ● How does your heart feel knowing in the midst of these unknowns that you are deeply loved, fully known, and tenderly cared for by God?

   _____

   _____

   _____

Take heart, friend. The same God who showed Himself faithful and mighty and ever-present in Joseph's life will show Himself to be the very same things for you. He is now and forever unchanging.

> "Jesus Christ is the same yesterday and today and forever."
> **Hebrews 13:8**

DAY 2
STUDY AND REFLECT

Today we're going to reflect on chapter 8 of the book *Forgiving What You Can't Forget.* If you haven't already read chapter 8, please do so before you begin.

1. Please read the book excerpt below and then answer the questions that follow.

"Grieving is dreaming in reverse.

When you think better days are ahead, you say things like, 'I dream of one day being a wife and mom, or an actress, or a chef, or a scientist.' Or, 'I dream of one day opening my own coffee shop, or writing a book, or going back to school.'"

But when you are grieving over something or someone that was taken away, you wish you could go back in time. You dream in reverse.

Instead of hoping for what will one day be, you long for a more innocent time when you lived more unaware of tragedy. But the griever knows they can't go back in time. So healing feels impossible, because circumstances feel unchangeable." (*Forgiving What You Can't Forget*, page 109)

So often we only think of grieving in terms of the death of a loved one. But we can grieve the loss of relationships, the loss of a dream, the loss of what we thought our life would look like.

What are you grieving in your life because of the choices others have made?

How is the unchangeable nature of what others have said or done impacting your ability to make progress in your life? Take some time to explain why. (Examples of progress: healing, peace, forgiveness, etc.)

2. Unchangeable can feel unforgivable. And we can find ourselves wondering why we should even bother going through the deep work of forgiveness if it won't make any kind of a difference. Below are several situations that can leave us feeling as if forgiveness is surely impossible. Read through this list and check all that apply to situations you are facing with people who have hurt you.

_____ They can't or aren't willing to cooperate with forgiveness.

_____ They refuse to stop their bad behaviors.

_____ They are no longer alive.

_____ Contacting them would be dangerous.

_____ You don't even know how to contact them.

_____ You're afraid they will want a restored relationship and that does not feel possible on your end.

_____ They don't think they need to be forgiven, so approaching them would only mean chaos.

Is there anything else you would add to this list?

ase read the book excerpt below and then answer the questions that
ilow.

> "Forgiveness releases to the Lord your need for them to be
> punished or corrected, giving it to the only One who can
> do this with right measures of justice and mercy.
>
> Forgiveness doesn't let the other person off the
> hook. It actually places them in God's hands."
> (*Forgiving What You Can't Forget*, pages 111–112)

Look up the following verses and summarize them in your own words:

Leviticus 19:18: _____

Proverbs 20:22: _____

Proverbs 24:29: _____

Romans 12:17–19: _____

What are some of the reasons we might struggle with releasing into God's
hands the people who have hurt us the deepest?

Why would it be dangerous for God to allow us to carry out our own ideas
of vengeance, especially when our wounds are still feeling quite raw?

Who would you want addressing your sin and your mistakes—our merciful
God or the person you have intentionally or unintentionally hurt?

Why should we actually be deeply grateful God says vengeance is His?

4. We don't have to see the justice of God playing out to know that it exists. And only God knows how to balance mercy, justice, and consequences appropriately. Look up Deuteronomy 32:4 and Psalm 11:7 to see why we can trust God to handle things rightly.

How does it comfort you or challenge you to know that the God who loves justice also deeply cares about people?

5. Please read the book excerpt below.

> "Sin always masquerades as fun and games. But pull back the curtain of the deceived human heart, and what you'll find hiding there will drive you to your knees to pray for that person. And maybe that's the very reason God instructs us to pray for our enemies." (*Forgiving What You Can't Forget*, pages 113-115)

Proverbs is a book of the Bible that makes it incredibly clear that sin comes with consequences. Read the passages of Scripture from Proverbs listed below in your Bible and then answer the questions that follow.

Proverbs 1:30–33
Proverbs 5:21–23
Proverbs 11:21

Where has it looked like the people who have sinned against you are just getting off the hook?

How do you feel knowing that there are consequences even if you cannot see those consequences?

6. "But I tell you, love your enemies and pray for those who persecute you." Matthew 5:44

The people who have hurt us are suffering from both past and present pain. How might praying for them actually soften our hearts toward them? (Feel free to also use the space below to actually write out a prayer for someone you are struggling to forgive.)

"Be kind and compassionate to one another, forgiving each other, just as in Christ God forgave you." Ephesians 4:32

Walter L. Liefeld shares that forgiveness is so much more than simply "letting bygones be bygones" in his New Testament commentary series.

"Forgiveness is not merely dismissing something out of mind, trying to forget it or overlooking it. A great deal of harm can be done not only when Christians perpetuate resentful attitudes against those who have wronged them but also when they sweep these wrongs 'under the carpet,' where they stay unresolved. We must face our own attitudes as well as the wrongs of others. If we truly forgive another that means putting an end to the matter by forgiving just as God has forgiven us, acknowledging the wrong and its effect on us, and then dismissing it, no longer pressing judgment and never calling it back to mind. Jesus taught that it is the person who has been forgiven much who loves much (Lk 7:47). It helps us to forgive others to remember how much God has forgiven us and the price that was paid. True forgiveness will mean that even if in our humanity we cannot completely forget the actions and effects that someone's sin caused, we can forgive the sin itself and refrain from allowing it to affect our estimation of that person."[12]

7. Let's finish up today by asking God to help us look at our lives from a fresh perspective.

While there are absolutely unchangeable facts about our situations, there are also changeable possibilities. For example, it's unchangeable when someone speaks hurtful statements to you. Those words can't be "unspoken." But you can be empowered to know that you get to decide how that unchangeable fact changes you—for good or bad. That unchangeable thing can be used to grow you more into the person you want to be or diminish you into someone you are not.

Fill in the left side of the chart below with some of the unchangeable facts you're currently struggling to deal with. Then ask God to help you fill in the two columns to the right with changeable possibilities. How might this fact change you in negative ways? How could it change you for good? How might God be glorified even in this? You get to choose.

UNCHANGEABLE FACT	POSSIBLE NEGATIVE OUTCOME	POSSIBLE POSITIVE OUTCOME
Hurtful statements were spoken to me.	I can let those words diminish me and cause me to become someone I am not.	I can ask God what He would say to me in light of those words and grow more into the person I want to be.

We can't change what's happened in the past. But we can decide how we move forward into our future.

STUDY AND REFLECT

Today we're going to reflect on chapter 9 of the book *Forgiving What You Can't Forget.* If you haven't already read chapter 9, please do so before you begin.

1. Please read the book excerpt below and then answer the questions that follow.

> "When someone is making destructive choices, it's usually because they are hurting. As I've stated over and over, hurting people will hurt other people. When we recognize this, we can invest our energy in one of two directions.
>
> The first direction is, we can draw appropriate boundaries. This is not to shut people out, but rather to shield ourselves from the consequences of their hurtful behaviors affecting us more than them.
>
> The other direction is to try and change that person, who, by the way, will only grow more and more difficult with every tightening grip of your attempted control. And even if you were successful, the most you could ever accomplish is behavior management." (*Forgiving What You Can't Forget*, page 123)

Where would you say you fall on this continuum when you see the people you love making destructive choices?

—|—|—|—|—|—|—|—|—|—|—|—|—|—|—

I draw and stick to
healthy, needed
boundary lines.

I panic and try
to control their
attitudes and actions.

2. Please read the book excerpt below and then answer the questions that follow.

> "I wish with every fiber of my being I could tell you that you can do enough to one day cause that person to change . . . to give enough . . . to love enough . . . to forgive enough . . . to beg enough . . . to talk enough . . . or to control enough. But it's not true. Change can only happen for them from the inside out. Truly sustainable, lasting change must come from inside their own heart, not from pressure exerted from the outside in." (*Forgiving What You Can't Forget*, pages 125–126)

Why might we as Christians fall easily into the trap of thinking it's our job to rescue others?

How does the idea of setting up boundaries make you feel? Does it leave you with positive feelings—"This makes me feel safe, sane, and secure"? Or does it stir up negative feelings—"I feel like I'm being unkind, unloving, and unfeeling"?

After reading this chapter, where do you see that setting up boundaries can be one of the most loving things you can do for yourself and others? Write out some of the possible benefits for everyone involved in the separate spaces provided below.

You:

Others:

3. Please read the book excerpt below and then answer the questions that follow.

"Boundaries aren't to push others away. They are to hold me together.

"Otherwise, I will downgrade my gentleness to hastily spoken words of anger and resentment. I will downgrade my progress with forgiveness to bitterness. I will downgrade my words of sincerity to frustrated words of anger, aggression, or rude remarks. I will downgrade my attitude for reconciliation to acts of retaliation . . . not because I'm not a good person but because I'm not a person keeping appropriate boundaries." (*Forgiving What You Can't Forget*, page 132)

When in your life has a lack of boundaries caused you to "downgrade" your words, your attitude, or your actions, all because you felt pushed beyond your capacity?

Proverbs 31:25–26 reads,

> "She is clothed with strength and dignity;
>   she can laugh at the days to come.
> She speaks with wisdom,
>   and faithful instruction is on her tongue."

When has a lack of boundaries led you to dread the days ahead?

How might setting boundaries better equip us to live out Proverbs 31:25–26?

4. Read Galatians 1:10 and Proverbs 29:25, and then answer the questions that follow.

What are some ways people-pleasing can play into our inability to set boundaries?

Who are the people that you feel pressured to keep happy? Are these the same people who would cause you to struggle with consistently keeping your boundaries?

Was there anything that surprised you about these verses? What do you need to take note of personally?

From the verses above, what wisdom can we gain about setting boundaries, especially in light of trying to keep everyone happy with us?

5. Please read the book excerpt below and then answer the questions that follow.

"I want them saved, but I am not their Savior. I want them to get better, but I cannot work harder at that than they can. They need Jesus. They need self-control. So, I shift from efforts of control to efforts of compassion." (*Forgiving What You Can't Forgive*, page 126)

> "Salvation is found in no one else, for there is no other name under heaven given to mankind by which we must be saved." **Acts 4:12**

What might it look like to try to play the role of Savior, Redeemer, and Rescuer in someone else's life?

Ask God to help you take an honest look at your relationships. Is there anyone you have overstepped boundaries with and are now trying to be their Savior?

6. Please read the book excerpt below and then answer the questions that follow.

> "Remember, forgiveness shouldn't be an open door for people to take advantage of us. Forgiveness releases our need for retaliation, not our need for boundaries."
> (*Forgiving What You Can't Forget*, page 127)

How might we be tempted to think that forgiveness and boundaries can't coexist in a relationship?

What are your thoughts on implementing boundaries after finishing this week of study?

Forgiveness is a must, but it's okay to take time to rebuild trust.

While forgiveness is unlimited and unconditional, reconciliation is limited and conditional based on repentance, the other person's willingness to be discipled, and their humility in the restoration process. If you still don't feel sure about how and where to set boundaries in your relationships, don't try to figure it out on your own. Ask the Lord for guidance. Find a trusted Christian counselor. Speak to people who are godly and wise. And know that sometimes, you may have to let people you love have their journey on one side of the street and have yours on the other side of the street for a while.

In the back of the *Forgiving What You Can't Forget* book, you will find a section called "What the Bible Actually Says About Forgiveness" with Scripture on when reconciliation isn't wise or possible. You will also find a section called "Some Important Notes to Consider on Abuse" at the back of that book. You are loved, you are not alone, and you don't have to walk through this without help.

DAYS 4 & 5
REVIEW AND READ

Use this time to go back and complete any of the study and reflection questions from previous days this week that you weren't able to finish. Make note of any revelations you've had and reflect on any growth or personal insights you've gained.

Spend the next two days reading chapters 10–11 of *Forgiving What You Can't Forget.* Use the space below to make note of anything in the chapters that stands out to you or encourages your heart.

Schedule

WEEK 5

BEFORE GROUP MEETING	Read Chapters 10–11 *Forgiving What You Can't Forget* Book
GROUP MEETING	View Video Session 5: The Compounding Effect of Unforgiveness Group Discussion Pages 120–125
PERSONAL STUDY DAY 1	Pages 126–131
PERSONAL STUDY DAY 2	Pages 132–136
PERSONAL STUDY DAY 3	Pages 137–143
DAYS 4 & 5 BEFORE WEEK 2 GROUP MEETING	Read Chapters 12–14 *Forgiving What You Can't Forget* Book Complete Any Unfinished Personal Study Activities

THE COMPOUNDING EFFECT OF

Unforgiveness

SESSION 5

WELCOME AND OPENING REFLECTION:

(SUGGESTED TIME: 15–20 MINUTES)

Welcome to session 5 of *Forgiving What You Can't Forget*.

Leader Note: Have a few people share their response to this question before starting the video:

What was your most helpful takeaway from this week's homework?

VIDEO (15:00 MINUTES)

Leader Note: Play the video segment for session 5.

THIS WEEK'S STATEMENT TO HOLD ONTO:

It's hard to be fruitful while we're holding onto what's hurtful.

VIDEO NOTES

Use the outline below to help you follow along with the teaching video or to take additional notes on anything that stands out.

Unforgiveness will have a compounding effect in our life and in the lives of those we interact with . . . far beyond what we even know.

Future generations will be impacted by our choice today to forgive or to not forgive.

Exodus 1:6–7: "Now Joseph and all his brothers and all that generation died, but the Israelites were exceedingly fruitful; they multiplied greatly, increased in numbers and became so numerous that the land was filled with them."

Exodus 1:8–11a:

- Israelites placed in Egyptian slavery
- Future connection = God eventually raises Moses up to deliver His people

Genesis 37:4, 8, 19–20:

- Joseph's brothers' hurt turns to hate.
- Their hatred and unforgiveness start a chain of events that lead an entire nation to be slaves in Egypt.

There's never just a little bit of hate. There's never just a little bit of unforgiveness. There's never just a little bit of bitterness.

When we make the decision to not forgive, it doesn't just affect us. There will be a multiplied impact that extends far wide, far reaching, more than we know.

Joseph's sons:

- Manasseh – Forgetful
- Ephraim – Fruitful

Genesis 50:20-26: Joseph dies in Egypt.

God's faithfulness doesn't mean we'll get everything we want. But it does mean God can still make our lives good.

Group DISCUSSION

(Suggested time: 40-45 minutes)

Leader Note: We have suggested questions to start with, but feel free to pick any of the additional questions as well. Consider the timeframe of your group and know the ultimate goal is meaningful discussion.

SUGGESTED QUESTIONS

1. We learned today there's never just a little bit of hate, unforgiveness, or bitterness. But our enemy Satan would love for us to believe otherwise. What are some of the excuses we may be tempted to make in order to hang onto our bitterness and anger?

2. Open your Bible to Proverbs 3:5-8 and have someone read it aloud. Our statement to hold onto is, "It's hard to be fruitful while we're holding onto what's hurtful." How is releasing our right to be offended an act of trust in God? How does this passage reinforce this idea of releasing what is hurtful so that we can be fruitful?

3. Joseph still had memories of his brothers' betrayal, but he refused to be held captive by those facts. Have you ever thought you had to fully forget to be able to freely forgive? How does it encourage you to know that it

is possible to live in freedom, even when you can still remember what happened?

4. Read Genesis 50:24–26. Joseph's life ended with him still in Egypt. How do we get to the place where we believe God's plans are still good even if they don't align with ours? Share how your own perspective has started to shift on this.

ADDITIONAL QUESTIONS (as time allows)

5. How were you impacted by hearing the connection between Joseph (who was a leader in Egypt) to Moses (who had to lead God's people out of slavery in Egypt), all because of Joseph's brothers' choice to hate?

6. Can you think of any other examples of the far-reaching impact of unforgiveness from your own life, Scripture, or even the history of our world?

7. Have someone read Galatians 6:7–9 aloud. What are some of the things we may reap from a life of sowing bitterness and unforgiveness? What kind of harvest can come from a life of releasing our hurts into the hands of God and sowing forgiveness instead?

CLOSING (SUGGESTED TIME: 5-MINUTES)

Leader Note: End your session by reading the "Between-Sessions Personal Studies" instructions to the group and making sure there are no questions pertaining to the homework. Then take a few minutes to pray over your group, either reading the provided prayer aloud over them or praying your own prayer.

BETWEEN-SESSIONS PERSONAL STUDIES

Every session in the *Forgiving What You Can't Forget Study Guide* includes five days of personal study to help you make meaningful connections between your life and what you're learning each week. This week, you'll work with the material in chapters 10–11 of the book *Forgiving What You Can't Forget.* You'll also have time to read chapters 12–14 of the book in preparation for your next group meeting.

PRAYER

Father God, we're so thankful that You are never dismissive of our pain. You meet us in it. You love us in the midst of it. But You also don't want us to stay stuck in it. Please show us the places where we're excusing bitterness and unforgiveness in our lives. Please help us to release every painful detail to You. We don't want to live our lives enslaved to the facts of what happened to us. It is for freedom You set us free, and that is how we want to live. Free. Healed. Whole. Teach us in the coming days what it means to live both fruitful and forgetful. We love You, we trust You, and we need You. In Jesus' name, amen.

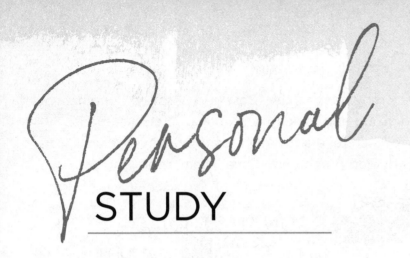

Personal STUDY

DAY 1
STUDY AND REFLECT

Today we're going to reflect more on the video. This will give us a good framework for digging into chapters 10 and 11 of the book *Forgiving What You Can't Forget* in the days that follow.

1. Open up your Bible and read Genesis 41:50-56.

    We learned in the video this week that Joseph named his sons Manasseh and Ephraim, names that mean "forgetful" and "fruitful."

    According to the passage of Scripture we just read, why does Joseph say he named his firstborn Manasseh?

    What reason does he give for naming his second son Ephraim?

Considering the fact that Joseph's children were born *before* the famine hit, we know Joseph had not yet seen his brothers or heard any kind of apology from them. How does this make Joseph's choice of names even more meaningful?

2. Sometimes we can get so focused on wanting God to deliver us from our circumstances, our land of suffering, that we forget He still wants to work in us and through us in the midst of them. What are some ways God could use you right where you are to be a blessing and a help to others?

Becoming "forgetful" about what his brothers did to him didn't justify their actions; it set Joseph free. Ask yourself these questions and then write out your thoughts in the space below.

How might my refusal to stop recalling, retelling, and ruminating on all the details of my pain actually be keeping me bound?

How might holding onto what is hurtful actually be making it harder for me to be fruitful in this season?

3. Fruit doesn't just show up in what we do. It also shows up in what we say. As we continue through this journey, it's important for us to pay attention to the words we speak.

   Read the passages of Scripture below and then answer the questions that follow:

   "With the tongue we praise our Lord and Father, and with it we curse human beings, who have been made in God's likeness. Out of the same mouth come praise and cursing. My brothers and sisters, this should not be. Can both fresh water and salt water flow from the same spring? My brothers and sisters, can a fig tree bear olives, or a grapevine bear figs? Neither can a salt spring produce fresh water." James 3:9–12

   "A good man brings good things out of the good stored up in his heart, and an evil man brings evil things out of the evil stored up in his heart. For the mouth speaks what the heart is full of." Luke 6:45

   Our hearts are a storehouse. And we are either speaking from the stored-up hurt of our heart or the hope of our soul. Stored-up hurt does need to be voiced for the purpose of healthy processing. But when it is voiced for the purpose of hurting others or weaponizing our pain, that's where unhealth is revealed. What are some healthy, safe ways to process the hurt in your heart?

Is there a situation currently in your life where your words are revealing unprocessed hurt and resentment? If so, what is one healthy choice you could make today to start making progress?

4. How often do you find yourself going back over the details of your most hurtful offenses with other people? (Please note: This does not mean within the confines of counseling, which we highly recommend. This is a question about how often we nurse and rehearse old wounds in general conversation.)

_____ I rarely feel the need to bring it up.

_____ I only talk about it when someone else asks.

_____ I only talk about it with my counselor/mentor/pastor/closest trusted friend.

_____ I seek out people who will sit and rehash every detail with me.

_____ I find myself trying to work it into any and every conversation.

5. Let's think about all of this in light of the truth we find in Ephesians 4:29-31: "Do not let any unwholesome talk come out of your mouths, but only what is helpful for building others up according to their needs, that it may benefit those who listen. And do not grieve the Holy Spirit of God, with whom you were sealed for the day of redemption. Get rid of all bitterness, rage and anger, brawling and slander, along with every form of malice."

Notice the verse doesn't say "Do not let any talk come out of your mouths . . ." It states, "Do not let any *unwholesome* talk come out of your mouths." The original Greek word for *unwholesome* is **saprós** and is used to describe decaying fruit that's no longer good to eat. The idea is that these words are not working toward a healthy or redemptive purpose. They are not just offensive; they are unproductive.[13]

That's why it's important to check the motive of our hearts and the purpose of our words. Is our motive for speaking these words "seeking healing" or "perpetuating hurt"? Is the purpose of our words necessary for processing and healing or venting to just get something that's hurt us off our chest and rally others to our side? Is there a current situation you could apply this verse to?

One other thing to note in the Ephesians passage is the phrase "do not grieve the Holy Spirit of God, with whom you were sealed for the day of redemption." What does this really mean? Paul uses the word *grieve* with great intentionality to remind us that God is not impersonal but intimately involved. This verse is used to remind us that our words can in fact cause heartache and sadness to God, a reality that we find also in the Old Testament (Isaiah 63:9–14). Disunity, strife, and slander grieve the Holy Spirit. Unity, oneness, and brotherly love bring honor to the Holy Spirit.

How does this speak to you?

Here are some additional questions we can ask ourselves to determine the motive of our heart and purpose of our speech before we share the details of our story:

- Are the words I'm about to speak going to be beneficial or detrimental to the listener?

- Do I sincerely need to process something with a good friend or am I just trying to rally someone else to my side?

- Will the words I'm about to speak grieve the Holy Spirit in any way?

- Is there anything I'm about to say in the heat of the moment now that I might regret later?

- Would it be a better use of my time and energy to talk with Jesus and ask Him to walk with me through the process of forgiveness?

Which question do you find most convicting and why?

FIGURING OUT FORGIVENESS

One of the ways we will know we are healing is by how we tell our story. When the details of how we were wronged are still the focal point and are presented like proof in a court case, where there is still a victim and an offender, chances are we are still hurting more than healing.

But when we tell the story and there's purpose to our pain, there's compassion for all involved, and the point of telling our story is sharing experiential wisdom that helps those listening— that's evidence of healing. That's when we know we've traded our **proof** for **perspective**.

Those listening are not having their curiosity satisfied with all the gory details of what happened but instead are gaining life lessons that will benefit them when facing similar situations. And we can begin to see we are truly moving forward in a healthy, godly way.

Pay attention to your words in the coming weeks.

Let even the smallest hint of healing in your words be cause for celebration. And when painful words come spilling out yet again? Sit with them instead of feeling condemned by them. Write them down in your journal and ask Jesus to help you follow the clues to where you still need healing within.

STUDY AND REFLECT

Today we're going to reflect on chapter 10 of the book *Forgiving What You Can't Forget.* If you haven't already read chapter 10, please do so before you begin.

Sometimes our stories will take the most unexpected twists and turns through the darkest valleys we've ever known—much like Joseph's story that we've learned about over the past two weeks.

This is often when we start suggesting to God all the ways He could surely fix our circumstances. Heal our hearts. Make things right.

But God loves us too much to do things our way. And His plan is always better even if we can't understand or see it clearly as it's unfolding.

Does this mean we stop praying? Not at all. Nor do we stop hoping and believing. But there is one thing we must shift our perspective on . . .

We must believe that God has a plan even if He's not at all lining things up like we wish He would. We must stop believing that *our* way of getting to the other side of our circumstances is the *only* way. God has a perfect plan for a path to a renewed joy and a redeemed future that's probably one we can't even fathom.

Let's ask God to help us start this week with hearts like Joseph's—hearts of surrender and obedient trust . . .

1. Please read the book excerpt below and then answer the questions that follow.

> "Webster's gives this definition of hope: 'It's a feeling of expectation and a desire for certain things to happen.'[14] But have you ever heard someone say they are just trying to 'keep hope alive'? It sounds more like a patient on life support than a promise on standby. The more I felt like hope was a risk rather than an assurance, the more I became afraid of the word rather than comforted by it.

To say I had hope felt like I was risking something on God's behalf that could make us both look incredibly foolish. I wouldn't dare verbalize it that bluntly. But when you are living out a story that makes no human sense at all, fear seems like the most rational of all internal commentaries. So 'hoping' meant hurting even more with every passing, unchanged moment." (*Forgiving What You Can't Forget*, page 141)

How do you feel about the idea of "hope" in your own life right now? Are you afraid to hope? Tired of hoping? Hanging onto it tooth and nail? Write out your honest thoughts below.

2. Please read the book excerpt below and then answer the questions that follow.

"God could see all of this. God could see my hurt, disillusionment, utter confusion, and desperate need for help. I absolutely believed in Him. But that became part of the problem. Because I'd seen Him do powerful things in my life before, miraculous things, I had astounding evidence of His faithfulness.

So, why did every request I made with my marriage seem to go absolutely unheard?

It was especially maddening when I felt like I had done everything I could to completely set the scene for God to move." (*Forgiving What You Can't Forget*, page 143)

Where in your life do you feel like your prayers are going unheard?

3. Read the following passages of Scripture in your Bible. Write out any words or phrases that describe what God does when you bring Him your prayers.

Psalm 40:1: _____

Psalm 116:1–2: _____

Psalm 6:8–9: _____

Let's look a little closer. The Hebrew word for *turned* in both Psalm 40:1 and Psalm 116:2 is **natah**, and it means "to stretch out, extend, spread out, pitch, turn, pervert, incline, bend, bow." [15] And then the Hebrew word for *accepts* in Psalm 6:9 is **laqach** and can mean "to take, get, fetch, lay hold of, seize, receive." [16] So not only does God hear our prayers, He turns and leans in close to listen. And not only does the God of the universe listen to us closely, He takes our prayers in His hands.

How do you need to let these truths comfort you today?

4. Please read the book excerpt below and then answer the questions that follow.

> "If we try and draw conclusions from the well of our deep pain, we will only have the sorrow of today to sip from. If, however, we draw strength from the deep well of God's promises for tomorrow and His faithfulness to us in the past, His living water is the goodness that will seep life into our dry and weary souls." (*Forgiving What You Can't Forget*, page 150)

Where would you say you have been drawing conclusions from—your well of pain or the deep well of God's promises?

Below you will find several truths about God's faithfulness on the left side of the page. Draw a line to connect each truth with the appropriate Scripture reference on the right.

TRUTH	SCRIPTURE
Even if we are faithless, God remains faithful.	Psalm 36:5
God is faithful in all He does.	1 Thessalonians 5:23–24
His faithfulness reaches through all generations.	2 Timothy 2:13
His faithfulness reaches to the skies.	Psalm 91:4
His faithfulness is a shield to us.	Psalm 33:4
He is faithful to sanctify and keep us.	Psalm 119:90

Which truth about His faithfulness do you most need today?

5. Tracing God's hand of faithfulness from yesterday truly does remind us that, even if we can't see His hand of activity today, He is here and He is faithful. Where has He been faithful to you in the past and how can you let this strengthen you today? Write about it in the space below.

6. We will all have seasons of sorrow in our lives, but no season of sorrow will last forever. Whether our tears are fully dried over these circumstances on this side of heaven or in eternity when God Himself wipes away every tear (Revelation 21:4), we can trust that sorrow has a stopping point.

   Look up these passages of Scripture and write out what you discover about God and sorrow.

   Psalm 30:5: _____

   Psalm 30:11: _____

   Psalm 119:28: _____

   John 16:22: _____

7. Even if we can't see how God is moving, even if we still feel stuck in our sorrow, even if we don't feel like we know what we're supposed to do . . . forgiveness is always healing in the right direction.

   Thinking back to the video teaching this week, how is choosing unforgiveness moving us in the wrong direction? How might that choice affect not just you but the people in your life and future generations? (Feel free to read back through your notes.)

   Write any last thoughts you have for today here.

STUDY AND REFLECT

Today we're going to reflect on chapter 11 of the book *Forgiving What You Can't Forget.* If you haven't already read chapter 11, please do so before you begin.

1. Please read the book excerpt below and then answer the questions that follow.

> "Getting hurt by people is hard. Getting hurt by what God allows can feel unbearable. While I might phrase my disillusionment as a question of why or how, when I lay my head on my tear-soaked pillow, questions can turn into bitter feelings. I probably wouldn't want to raise my hand at Bible study and admit I'm honestly struggling to forgive God, but I have questions around this. I have hurt feelings. Maybe you do too." (*Forgiving What You Can't Forget*, page 156)

How does this quote resonate with you?

Where are you feeling frustrated and confused by what God has allowed in your life or where He hasn't moved like you wanted Him to?

2. Please read the book excerpt below and then answer the questions that follow.

> "Since trust in relationships is built in part with good communication, then more effectively praying has to play a role in my trust with God. I've been praying for almost as long as I've been living. But I've very rarely had the thought to look around at my life and see today, this moment, in this season, as the answered prayer.

When I think about prayer requests, I think of what I 'hope' God will do . . . not what 'has been done' for today.

The reason I miss seeing what I'm living today as the answer to my prayers is that very often, maybe even always, it's not what I thought it would be. God's answers don't look like what I have pictured so clearly in my mind." (*Forgiving What You Can't Forget*, page 159)

Which of these best describes your prayer life:

_____ An honest conversation with a God who loves me but ultimately knows best

_____ Tossing a penny in a fountain and hoping for the best

_____ Placing an online order and looking for it in record time

_____ Other:_____

Taking into consideration all that you've learned in chapter 11, how would you like your prayer life to change?

3. We are living answered prayers today. Think through the three different types of provision in the chapter and answer the questions below.

   Loaf from an oven (Leviticus 2:4) – This is when God's provision looks like what we want or expect.

   Where have you seen "loaf" provision in your life recently?

Manna from heaven (Deuteronomy 8:3) – This is provision that consistently comes from God, but that we can't control in any way.

Where have you seen "manna" provision?

Jesus who declared Himself as the bread of life (John 6:35) – This is provision in Christ deposited inside of us that nourishes and sustains us all the way down to our souls.

Where has Jesus shown up as "bread of life" provision for you today?

> "If we have Jesus today, we are living in answered prayer and perfect provision."
> (*Forgiving What You Can't Forget*, page 162)

4. Having a biblically informed view of God impacts our willingness to trust Him. Read the passages of Scripture below and then answer the questions that follow.

> ". . . your Father knows what you need before you ask him."
> **Matthew 6:8b**

> "If you, then, though you are evil, know how to give good gifts to your children, how much more will your Father in heaven give good gifts to those who ask him!" **Matthew 7:11**

> "Every good and perfect gift is from above, coming down from the Father of the heavenly lights, who does not change like shifting shadows." **James 1:17**

Where might God not be answering a prayer in your life the way you want? How could you step out in faith and trust that He knows what you truly need right now is something different or that He wants you to find your hope and sufficiency in Him?

How can combining the knowledge that God knows what you need and He is by His very nature a giver of good gifts help you trust Him as you wait on Him to answer your prayers?

5. Trusting God doesn't mean we won't ever want things to be different in our lives. It also doesn't mean we can't ask Him to change our situation.

   Open up your Bible and read Mark 14:32–36.

   How does it comfort you to know that even Jesus asked God to change His circumstances and fix what God surely could have fixed in an instant?

   Write out the last nine words of Jesus' prayer from Mark 14:36.

   Why do you think Jesus was able to pray with this level of trust and surrender before going to the cross?

Are these nine words ones you feel that you could sincerely pray right now? Write out your reasons why or why not in the space below.

6. Please read the book excerpt below and then answer the questions that follow.

> "Sometimes people can have hidden agendas and skewed motives. Sometimes people lie. Sometimes people don't seek a greater good. But none of this is true about God. He is good. He is the only source of making anything good out of everything in front of me. Trusting God with all of this is what my soul was made to do. I guess it just takes time for my battered heart and my prone-to-fear mind to catch up." (*Forgiving What You Can't Forget*, page 168)

When have you experienced a breach of trust with another person so deep that it led to a breakdown in your trust with God?

Part of rebuilding trust with God is knowing and believing He is nothing like the people who have hurt us. Truthfully, even the very best people in our lives pale in comparison to God in all of His wisdom and kindness, His love and majesty, His holiness and goodness.

Look up the passages of Scripture below and use them to finish this sentence: People may _____ , but God _____. (The first example has been done for you.)

Hebrews 10:23:

People may __break their promises to me__ , but God __will always keep His promises__ .

Numbers 23:19:

People may _____, but God

_____ .

Psalm 9:10:

People may _____, but God

_____ .

Hebrews 13:8:

People may _____, but God

_____ .

Are there any other "People may, but God" statements you would add?

7. Please read the book excerpt below and then answer the questions that follow.

> "I now realize God doesn't need to be forgiven.
>
> He hasn't wronged me.
>
> He hasn't sinned.
>
> I was just looking at the hardest place and thinking it was the end. I missed something so important. Something I now see. What things look like from an earthly perspective God sees differently.
>
> I kept seeing what I'd lost, the damage, the hurt, the pain. I was blinded to the fact that I don't know all there is, what's really best and what is not. And though the days were awful, I was not without God.
>
> Every day He was providing for me. Every day He was there. And whether I could recognize it or not, I was living in answered prayers." (*Forgiving What You Can't Forget*, pages 169–170)

Finish out today prayerfully considering this excerpt from the book. Do you feel as though you can land in the same place, with these same conclusions in your current circumstances? Where do you need God to continue helping you make peace with what you're going through? Remember, God is okay with your wrestling and your questions. And He would much rather you press in close to Him than completely pull away. Journal your thoughts on this in the space below.

DAYS 4 & 5
REVIEW AND READ

Use this time to go back and complete any of the study and reflection questions from previous days this week that you weren't able to finish. Make note of any revelations you've had and reflect on any growth or personal insights you've gained.

Spend the next two days reading chapters 12–14 of *Forgiving What You Can't Forget.* Use the space below to make note of anything in the chapters that stands out to you or encourages your heart.

Schedule

Week 6

BEFORE GROUP MEETING	Read Chapters 12–14 *Forgiving What You Can't Forget* Book
FINAL GROUP MEETING	View Video Session 6: This Isn't Easy, But It Is Good Group Discussion Pages 146–152
PERSONAL STUDY DAY 1	Pages 153–159
PERSONAL STUDY DAY 2	Pages 160–165
PERSONAL STUDY DAY 3	Pages 165–172
PERSONAL WRAP-UP	Read the book of Philemon in your Bible

THIS ISN'T EASY, BUT IT IS

Good

SESSION 6

WELCOME AND OPENING REFLECTION:

(SUGGESTED TIME: 15–20 MINUTES)

Welcome to session 6 of *Forgiving What You Can't Forget*.

Leader Note: Have a few people share their response to this question before starting the video:

What was your most helpful takeaway from this week's homework?

VIDEO (21:00 MINUTES)

Leader Note: Play the video segment for session 6.

THIS WEEK'S STATEMENT TO HOLD ONTO:

We forgive people from the overflow of what we really believe to be true about Christ.

VIDEO NOTES

We are now forgiveness ambassadors.

2 Timothy 2:

- v. 15: workers approved by God
- v. 16: avoid godless chatter
- vv. 22–24 - "avoid foolish and stupid arguments" = "untrained argument"

We can't control what people do to us. But we can control how we react to these situations.

Philemon: a one-page book of the Bible that's a profound story of how forgiveness should play out.

Earthly Descriptions

PAUL: a pastor in prison and deeply invested friend writing a letter to Philemon on behalf of a bondservant named Onesimus

PHILEMON: recipient of the letter, master of Onesimus, friend of Paul and fellow Christian

ONESIMUS: Philemon's runaway bondservant

Eternal Perspectives

PAUL: a prisoner of Christ but also a reflection of Christ

PHILEMON: a man of faith and love and a great encourager

ONESIMUS: a man who becomes a Christian under Paul's influence

Reframing our perspective isn't denying our circumstances. It's gaining a better perspective through which to process our hardships.

2 Corinthians 10:3–5: ". . . we take captive every thought to make it obedient to Christ."

We must see people rightly and see Jesus rightly. This will help us see our situations rightly.

Philemon 1:8–9a: "Therefore, although in Christ I could be bold and order you to do what you ought to do, yet I prefer to appeal to you on the basis of love."

Our feelings matter, but feelings cannot be our guide. Only Truth can guide us.

To the extent that I believe Christ cares for me and is the Redeemer of my life is the extent that I will be able to live this message of forgiveness.

Philemon 1:15: Forgiveness cost Philemon a worker but gained him a brother.

When we hold onto anger, bitterness, and unforgiveness, we do the devil's work for him.

People sometimes don't care to meet our Jesus until they meet the beautiful reality of Jesus in our lives.

Group DISCUSSION

(*Suggested time:* 40–45 minutes)

Leader Note: We have suggested questions to start with, but feel free to pick any of the additional questions as well. Consider the timeframe of your group and know the ultimate goal is meaningful discussion.

SUGGESTED QUESTIONS

1. Have someone read Philemon 1:1, 4–7, 10–16 out loud. Paul not only tried to help Philemon view Onesimus through the lens of an eternal perspective, Paul also made sure to remind Philemon of who *he* was in Christ. How could forgetting who we are in Christ lead to us making poor choices in how we handle offense? Why is it important for us to make God-honoring choices even if no one else involved in our situation does?

2. We learned today that we treat people from the overflow of our thought life. Take some time to talk through these suggested questions that can help us take our thoughts captive. Which one feels the most personally challenging or convicting? Which perspective shift do you most need right now in a current situation you are dealing with?

   • Do we see the people involved as just a sum total of our earthly perspective of them or as Christ sees them?

- Do we see ourselves as the saint and them as the sinner or that we are all humans in need of Christ?

- Do we want to force our agenda or appeal to people on the basis of love?

- Do we believe that even if they don't do the right thing that Christ can still redeem this situation in our life?

- Am I willing to accept God's version of the good that could possibly be worked out for all parties involved even if it doesn't feel good to me right now?

3. Our statement to hold onto this week is: "We forgive people from the overflow of what we really believe to be true about Christ." Why might doubting Jesus' goodness or ability to take care of us cause us to withhold forgiveness? What things do you know to be true about Jesus that can actually help you to forgive?

4. This study has biblically trained us in how to forgive not just the big events of our life but also how to weave a forgiveness perspective into how we view everything we face. What is one of the truths you've learned in this Bible study that you believe will help you with the smaller, everyday offenses?

ADDITIONAL QUESTIONS (as time allows)

5. An ambassador by its simplest definition is "an authorized representative or messenger."[17] What are some of the things that may leave us feeling unqualified to be forgiveness ambassadors?

6. Open your Bible to Colossians 1:17–20 and read it out loud. According to this passage, why are we actually the perfect people to carry Christ's message of forgiveness and reconciliation to the world?

7. The difference in Austin before training for the Marines and afterward was significant and noticeable. What kind of changes might the world see in a person who goes from being stuck in their pain to allowing those places to actually become forgiveness training ground? What changes (big or small) have you noticed within yourself since you've started moving through this process of forgiveness?

8. What has been one of your favorite or most beneficial takeaways from this study for helping you process the deeper places of pain?

CLOSING (SUGGESTED TIME: 5-MINUTES)

Leader Note: End your session by reading the "Final Personal Studies" instructions to the group and making sure there are no questions pertaining to the homework. Then take a few minutes to pray over your group, either reading the provided prayer aloud over them or praying your own prayer.

FINAL PERSONAL STUDIES

Every session in the *Forgiving What You Can't Forget Study Guide* includes five days of personal study to help you make meaningful connections between your life and what you're learning each week. This week, you'll work with the material in chapters 12–14 of the book *Forgiving What You Can't Forget.* You'll also have time to study the book of Philemon.

PRAYER

Father God, thank You for this journey we've been on over the last six weeks. While this may be the end of us meeting to study together, we know this is just the beginning of a lifelong journey of choosing to bring the beauty of forgiveness to a broken and hurting world. We are so thankful we no longer have to be women controlled by the pain of our past. We're believing that, with You, we can live with peaceful hearts, uncluttered minds, and arms wide open with compassion. We want our lives to be evidence that Your Son Jesus is real. As Your forgiveness flows so freely to us, may it also flow freely through us. In Jesus' name, amen.

Personal STUDY

DAY 1
STUDY AND REFLECT

Today we're going to reflect on chapter 12 of the book *Forgiving What You Can't Forget.* If you haven't already read chapter 12, please do so before you begin.

It's so hard to believe this is our last week of studying God's Word side-by-side with *Forgiving What You Can't Forget.* You have pulled up a seat to the table and leaned into this hard but holy call to forgive.

Even if this process has felt incredibly messy, even if you feel like you have a long way to go, even if your heart still needs some convincing . . . may you hear the Father's most tender whisper over your willingness to come this far: "Well done, Daughter. Well done."

Let's continue to lean in and learn . . .

1. How have you been impacted by the painful loss of a loved one because of death, unexpected rejection, or even your own difficult, but needed, choice to distance yourself from them?

2. Please read the book excerpt below and then answer the questions that follow.

> "When your personal loss came because of another person's foolishness, selfishness, meanness, or irresponsibility, sorrow can quickly invite bitterness you didn't even know you were capable of. But instead of being just an invited visitor, bitterness wants to move right into your emptiness without permission. At the time you may not have even realized it or recognized what it was, because at first bitter feelings can feel quite justifiable and oddly helpful. Where sorrow has over time made us numb, bitterness at least allows us to feel something.
>
> But with time, bitterness doesn't just want to be something that awakens some feeling. It wants to become your only feeling. Bitterness doesn't just want to room with you; it wants to completely consume everything about you." (*Forgiving What You Can't Forget*, page 174)

Are there any places in your life where you can see how sorrow made a way for bitterness to enter your heart? (Your answers to question 1 may reveal some of those places.)

What are some of the excuses we might use to try to hold onto our bitter feelings?

Look up Proverbs 4:23, a verse we discussed earlier in the study in reference to Joseph's brothers who refused to address the hurt in their own hearts. How does this verse reaffirm the fact that there's no such thing as a little bit of bitterness and we must deal with it as soon as we see it?

3. Now we're going to look at a list of ways bitterness can play out in our own lives. As you read these indicators of hidden bitterness, remember

this isn't a sign of a hard heart. It's usually quite the opposite. When these indicators are apparent in one's life, it's usually because their heart was tender and got very hurt. As we learned before, there is no condemnation in Christ. (See Romans 8:1.) But we do need to leave room for the Holy Spirit's conviction. We can't address what we don't acknowledge.

Place a check mark beside each of the following indicators you see in yourself.

☐ Derogatory assumptions

☐ Sharp, cutting comments

☐ A grudge that feels increasingly heavy inside you

☐ The desire for the one that hurt you to suffer

☐ Anxiety around the unfairness of other people's happiness

☐ Skepticism that most people can't be trusted

☐ Cynicism about the world in general

☐ Negativity cloaked as you having a more realistic view than others

☐ Resentment toward others whom you perceive moved on too quickly

☐ Frustrations with God for not doling out severe enough consequences

☐ Seething anger over the unfairness of it all that grows more intense over time

☐ Obsessing over what happened by replaying the surrounding events over and over

☐ Making passive-aggressive statements to prove a point

☐ One-upping other people's sorrow or heartbreak to show your pain is worse

☐ Feeling justified in behaviors you know aren't healthy because of how wronged you've been

☐ Snapping and exploding on other people whose offenses don't warrant that kind of reaction

☐ Becoming unexplainably withdrawn in situations you used to enjoy

- ☐ Disconnecting from innocent people because of the fear of being hurt again
- ☐ Irrational assumptions of worst-case scenarios
- ☐ Demanding unrealistic expectations
- ☐ Refusing to tell the person who hurt you what's really bothering you
- ☐ Stiff-arming people who don't think the same way you do
- ☐ Rejecting opportunities to come together and talk about things
- ☐ Refusing to consider other perspectives
- ☐ Blaming and shaming the other person inside your mind over and over
- ☐ Covertly recruiting others to your side under the guise of processing or venting

4. Spend a little time processing your answers to the last question.

Is there anything on the list above that you didn't realize could be an indication of hidden bitterness?

Which indicators are you surprised to see in yourself?

We learned in this chapter that bitterness doesn't have a core of hate but of hurt. Do you see a clear connection between any of the indicators you checked and a past hurt? Write anything that comes to mind below. (And if not, it's okay. This is a continuing process. Ask the Lord to help you connect those dots so you can correct those dots.)

5. Read Psalm 73:21–26 in your Bible and then answer the questions that follow.

   We might think God pulls away from a heart that is filled with and acting on bitterness, but what do these verses say He does instead? List every detail you find from the verses.

   How do these truths comfort you as you begin addressing your own places of bitterness?

   Where do you most need God to be Your strength and Your portion at this point in your journey with living out forgiveness?

6. Not only does God stay with us in *our* grief, He calls us to sit with others in *their* grief. We see this truth in Romans 12:15 where Paul instructs us, "Rejoice with those who rejoice; mourn with those who mourn."

   We also find this call in the story of Job. Although Job's friends eventually do end up overstepping their boundaries—trying to make sense of Job's situation and speaking without grace or mercy into matters that were not theirs to enter into—they did set a good biblical example in how they first showed up.

   Look up Job 2:11–13 in your Bible. Write out some of the descriptions you find for how Job's friends sat with him in his grief.

Why might we be tempted to hold someone else's grief at a distance instead of living out the example given in this passage of Scripture?

We might think of grieving with others simply as our gift of love and compassion to them. What new insights did you gain from chapter 12, though, about how God can also use our willingness to sit with them to do a good work in us?

When has holding space for someone else's grief softened your heart?

> "What if bitterness is actually a seed of beautiful potential not yet planted in the rich soil of forgiveness?"
> (*Forgiving What You Can't Forget*, page 184)

7. Please read the book excerpt below and then answer the questions that follow.

> ". . . there is one sure way to know loss is part of someone's life—they are breathing.
>
> . . . if they have a beating heart, they are carrying loss of some kind. So be kind. Respect their loss. And, in doing so, it will make us more aware and soften our own propensity toward hardness.

This isn't to say we tolerate things we shouldn't or we allow abusive behavior or enable others' chaotic choices. But, instead of labeling them as bad or awful or toxic people, maybe we can just say, 'They are suffering from loss. Maybe they filled their loss with unkindness. God, help me not add to their pain or join their club. But, rather, let all of this teach me something.'" (*Forgiving What You Can't Forget*, pages 182–183)

Who or what in your life have you labeled chaotic, toxic, or awful?

Read through Colossians 3:12–14. What do you most need to "clothe" yourself with when it comes to these difficult people or situations?

Knowing now that bitterness has a core of hurt, how might remembering that sorrow and pain have deeply shaped who they are change the way you think about and interact with them?

Today is a good day to "sit" with someone else's grief in prayer, specifically the person's name you wrote above. Write out a prayer for that person in the space below, asking God to heal any bitterness caused by sorrow and allowing Him to soften your heart toward them as only He can.

DAY 2
STUDY AND REFLECT

Today we're going to reflect on chapter 13 of the book *Forgiving What You Can't Forget.* If you haven't already read chapter 13, please do so before you begin.

1. Please read the book excerpt below and then answer the questions that follow.

> "*Resentment* is usually attached to a specific person for a specific incident. *Bitterness* is usually the collective feeling of all our resentments. But however you define those words, they are part of the same problem.
>
> Bitterness isn't just a label we place on people and the feelings around the hurts they cause. It is like liquid acid seeping into every part of us and corrupting all it touches. It not only reaches unhealed places, but it also eats away at all that is healed and healthy in us. Bitterness leaves nothing unaffected. Bitterness over one thing will locate bitterness hiding inside of us over other things. It will always intensify our reactions, skew our perspective, and take us further and further away from peace." (*Forgiving What You Can't Forget,* pages 190–191)

Think back to a time when a seemingly small offense caused you to lose your cool in a big way. Write about that experience here.

How might that offense have actually been acting like a magnet, calling forth other feelings of undealt-with wrongs?

2. We learned today that our reactions are manipulated through the lens of unresolved past hurts. A bitter lens leads to a bitter reaction. Sometimes we don't realize that our out-of-proportion reactions with someone reveal we've been storing up a collection of resentments.

Who is most likely to stir up an ugly or out-of-proportion reaction from you?

How would you describe the collection of resentments you have stored up when it comes to this person or people? Large, small, continually growing?

Where do you see a connection between the resentments you are holding onto and the level of reaction you have toward these people?

3. Please read the book excerpt below.

> "Humanity rises up and demands that I be declared the right one, the good one, the victimized one. But never has that made anything better for me; it's only embittered me. Humility bows low and claims the greatest victory a human can ever grasp: God's prize of peace." (*Forgiving What You Can't Forget*, page 194)

It's important to remember that humility isn't a sign of weakness. It's actually a sign of great strength in your character and in your spiritual maturity. Scripture has much to say about humility. But one of the most powerful and beautiful pictures we find is of Jesus Himself in Philippians 2:1–11. Read through this passage in your Bible and answer the questions that follow.

How does this passage of Scripture describe humility?

Sometimes what hinders us from wanting to humble ourselves is feeling like we aren't the ones who have done anything wrong. Why did Jesus choose to humble Himself even though He had committed no sin and done no wrong? Do you think less of Jesus or more of Him because of His humble nature?

How does it speak to your heart to know that Jesus isn't asking us to do anything that He hasn't already done when He asks us to live lives of humility?

4. Romans 12:18 teaches, "If it is possible, as far as it depends on you, live at peace with everyone."

What is your first reaction to the idea that peace in our lives isn't being prevented by other people's choices . . . it's made possible by our own?

"If it is possible" reveals to us that there will be times when peace is not possible with another person. But then "as far as it depends on you" reminds us we are called to do our part. Read through Romans 12:14-21. Write out every peace-bringing instruction you find there in the space below.

Which ones do you most need the Lord to help you implement in your life and relationships right now?

FIGURING OUT FORGIVENESS

Living a life that reveals the evidence of Jesus within us will require us to surrender our offenses daily, keep our hearts swept clean of bitterness, and remain humble even when we are hurt.

This might sound like a lot of work, but let's not forget this reminder from the book:

". . . as hard as this seems, I think it's harder to keep letting circumstances and complicated people kidnap my peace. It's not just hurting me; it's hurting everyone. Remember how I said that bitterness leaks out like acid? The stain of bitterness doesn't end at the tips of my fingers . . . it leaks onto every person I touch." (*Forgiving What You Can't Forget*, pages 199–200)

Hebrews 12:15 reminds us that a "bitter root grows up to cause trouble and defile many."

Ask God to make your heart tender as you process through these questions:

- Do I want my relationship with my spouse to be defined by bitterness?

- Do I want my children defiled by my bitterness?

- Do I want my friends and family contaminated by my bitterness?

- Do I want my church relationships stained by my bitterness?

- Do I want my legacy to be one of bitterness?

Oh, friend. These can be some truly painful questions to consider. They are painful for me. But there comes a point where we must be honest with ourselves about how far-reaching and deeply impactful our undealt-with bitterness can be.

ead the book excerpt below and then answer the questions that

itterness is a bad deal that makes big promises on the front end but delivers nothing you really want on the back end. Only God has what I really want. Turning my heart over to bitterness is me turning away from God.

So, I bow low . . . not because I want to.

Because I need to. 'God, I give this situation to You. I release my evidence of all the reasons they were so wrong. I release my need to see this person punished. I release my need for an apology. I release my need for this to feel fair. I release my need for You to declare me right and them wrong. Show me what I need to learn from all of this. And then give me Your peace in place of my anger.'" (*Forgiving What You Can't Forget*, page 195)

What kind of promises has bitterness made to you?

How have the promises of bitterness proven to be hollow and unhelpful?

Now look up these passages of Scripture: Matthew 11:29–30; James 4:6-7, 10; and Proverbs 18:12.

What are some of the promises we find attached to bowing low and choosing humility?

6. What do you most need to release right now when it comes to the people who have hurt you? Check all that apply.

_____ My evidence

_____ My need to see this person punished

_____ My need for an apology

_____ My need for this to feel fair

_____ My need for God to declare me right and them wrong

Finish today by writing out your own prayer of release.

_____

_____

_____

_____

_____

_____

DAY 3
STUDY AND REFLECT

Today we're going to reflect on chapter 14 of the book *Forgiving What You Can't Forget.* If you haven't already read chapter 14, please do so before you begin.

1. Please read the book excerpt below and then answer the questions that follow.

> "Life is rarely tidy. Relationships aren't easy. And the constant stresses and strains of managing and navigating so many daily issues is hard on the human heart. I can find myself feeling like I'm doing really well with keeping my heart swept clean of bitterness one minute and the next minute feeling like a complete failure. When the same person I've worked hard to forgive does another thing that hurts me, I can be tempted to dig up my proof of what they did in the past, weaponize my pain against them and feel bitterness rush back inside of me like an unstoppable flood.

> But as I've sat with these feelings of hesitation and wrestling, I've come to the conclusion that the goal with forgiveness isn't perfection— it's progress." (*Forgiving What You Can't Forget*, page 207)

How do you feel you have been doing in this journey with forgiveness? Do you feel like you are learning and growing? Have you been frustrated by what has felt like setbacks and failures? Write your honest thoughts below.

What kind of freedom do you find in knowing that the goal is progress, *not* perfection?

2. We learned in this chapter that progress isn't the ability to never get hurt or offended; it's letting that pain drive us to new healing habits and perspectives. And we don't have to cooperate with forgiveness perfectly—just progressively—for it to be good.

   Check any of the small moments of progress below that you've seen in your own journey over the past few weeks. Even if you only check one, that's progress! Circle one you specifically would like the Lord to help you focus on over the next few days.

   _____ Have one better thought.

   _____ Have one better reaction.

   _____ Have one better way to process.

   _____ Have one better conversation.

   _____ Have one boundary you lovingly communicate and consistently keep.

   _____ Have one better choice to not reach for that substance to numb out.

_____ Have one better heart pivot toward forgiveness instead of resentment.

_____ Have one less day when you stay mad.

_____ Have one less hour when you refuse grace.

Is there anything else you would add to this list that has felt like progress in your own life and relationships? Write it out as a celebration of the work Jesus is doing in you.

Where in your life have you started seeing beautiful again, or at least the real hope of beauty? Share your thoughts here.

3. Please read the book excerpt below and then answer the questions that follow.

> "... I can't expect a perfection in others I'm not even capable of living out myself. I need grace for my very human tendencies and so do others.
>
> Confession breaks the cycle of chaos inside of me.
>
> Forgiveness breaks the cycle of chaos between us."
> (_Forgiving What You Can't Forget_, page 212)

What are some of the things that might cause us to try to avoid conviction and put off confession?

Read Matthew 7:3–5. Why must we stay aware of our own sinful nature and allow God to address those sins as we forgive and live in relationship with others?

4. A beautiful way to begin weaving this practice of letting God search our hearts for sin is using Psalm 19:12–14 and Psalm 139:23–24 as prayer guides. Read through these passages and then spend some time asking the Lord to convict you of any unconfessed sin in your heart. Journal in the space below knowing that God doesn't show us our sin to condemn us. He convicts us so He can restore us. Restoring us to right relationship with Him. Restoring us to joy. Restoring us to the plans and purposes He has for our life.

(For other encouraging passages on the benefits of repentance and confession, see 1 John 1:9; Psalm 51:7–12; and Acts 3:19.)

5. Please read the book excerpt below and then answer the questions that follow.

> "Maturity isn't the absence of hard stuff. Maturity is the evidence that a person allowed the hard stuff to work for them rather than against them." (*Forgiving What You Can't Forget*, page 214)

Read Romans 5:3–5 and James 1:2–4 in your Bible and then answer the questions that follow.

How is this journey with forgiveness producing perseverance in you?

Where do you see it changing your character for the good?

How has God been helping you place your hope in the right place and strengthening that hope within you?

What other benefits have you seen from the hardness of this process, either within you or even in some of your relationships?

6. How do we walk all of this out practically in our day-to-day lives?

One of the best ways to align our hearts with the spiritual maturity God wants us to have is to saturate our thinking and processing with the truths from His Word. The chart on page 171 will help us to not only ingest God's Word but to digest it, making it part of how we think and how we live.

Using the designed Bible study worksheets provided, follow the instructions to study and consider how to better live out a few of the suggested passges of Scripture.

Instructions:

1. You'll see there's a square in the center of the diagram where you can write the verse.

2. On the top of the square write the theme of this verse.

3. On the bottom of the square write the opposite of the theme.

4. On the left side of the square, in the top section of the allotted space, write out what God wants us to do in response to this verse.

5. On the bottom section of that divided left side, write out what the enemy wants us to do in response to this verse.

6. On the right side of the square, write out these words with space to journal a few lines under each word:

   - Progress—Where am I making progress with this verse?

   - Suppress—Is there a situation where I am wanting to ignore this verse?

   - Digress—Is there a situation where I'm taking steps backward with living this verse?

   - Regress—Where am I living in rebellion against this verse?

   - Confess—Now, I am aware of some confessions I need to make. (I write these out, asking God to give me a spirit of humility as I do this.)

   - Forgiveness—Where is someone not living this verse with me? (This is an opportunity for forgiveness.)

Here's an example of how this looked when I did this activity:

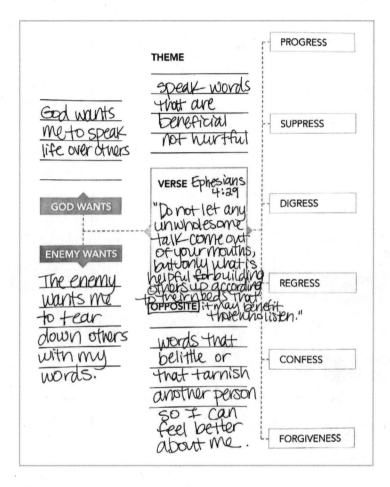

Go to proverbs31.org/forgiveness to get printable worksheets with this Bible study tool or copy the one on page 172 for personal use.

You will find a list of suggested passages of Scripture on page 217 in the *Forgiving What You Can't Forget* book that you can use for this exercise.

Other possible passages you can use:

Colossians 3:12	1 Peter 2:21–23	2 Timothy 2:16
Matthew 7:1–2	1 Peter 3:8	Proverbs 12:18
1 Peter 2:19	James 3:13	Proverbs 15:1
	Romans 12:19	

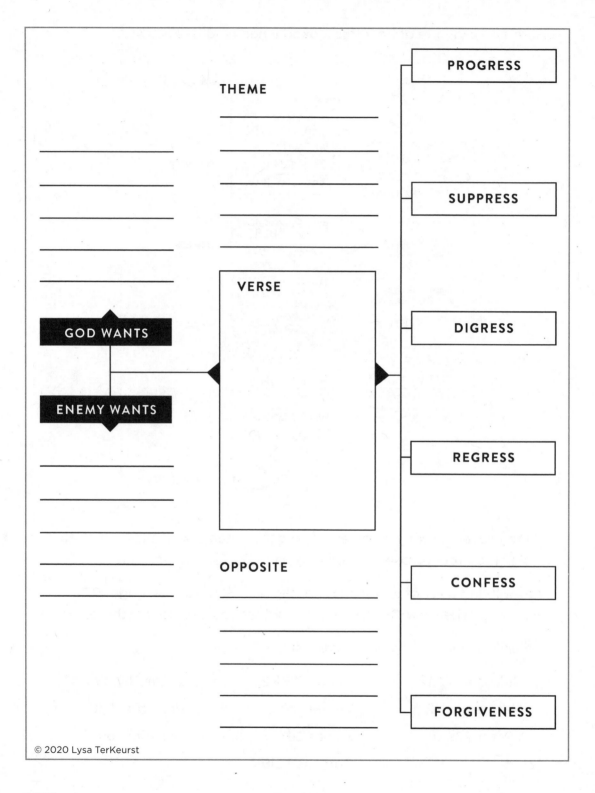

THEME

GOD WANTS

ENEMY WANTS

VERSE

OPPOSITE

PROGRESS

SUPPRESS

DIGRESS

REGRESS

CONFESS

FORGIVENESS

Just pick one per day to process. Please don't feel any pressure to do more. Also please realize this is just for you to process and internalize these verses for yourself. Don't fret if you are unsure of an answer . . . just keep going and ask God to reveal what He wants you to see. The focus here is on God's Word—not getting every blank filled in perfectly.

As we become more aware of what needs to be confessed and opportunities to practice forgiveness, we will become more mature. We'll become better wives, moms, friends, sisters, neighbors, bosses, employees, and daughters. We'll look more and more like Jesus as we live out His Word.

And while this may *look* like the end of our time together, it isn't. You'll find another day of study in the following pages, helping you learn more about becoming a forgiveness ambassador. And hopefully you will return to these pages again and again as a resource to help you in this continual process of forgiving.

As you finish up today's assignments, take a few moments to write out a prayer thanking God for all that He has taught you through this study, asking Him to continue healing and helping you, and committing to keep trusting Him that forgiveness is a beautiful gift to receive and to give.

PERSONAL WRAP-UP TIME WITH PHILEMON

Use this time to go back and complete any of the study and reflection questions from previous days this week that you weren't able to finish. Make note of any revelations you've had and reflect on any growth or personal insights you've gained. Also, have a marked moment where you go back and look at your answers to some of the questions from week one. Note where you see signs of progress and celebrate how far God has brought you.

Learning to Live as Forgiveness Ambassadors

> "All this is from God, who reconciled us to himself through Christ and gave us the ministry of reconciliation: that God was reconciling the world to himself in Christ, not counting people's sins against them. And he has committed to us the message of reconciliation. We are therefore Christ's ambassadors, as though God were making his appeal through us. We implore you on Christ's behalf: Be reconciled to God." **2 Corinthians 5:18–20**

Paul, who wrote the majority of the letters in the New Testament, is a true ambassador for Christ, a man trained to live the message of forgiveness. One of Paul's letters where he lives out this calling is in the book of Philemon. In this letter, Paul demonstrates how forgiveness can begin when we reframe how we see people using the eternal perspective of who they are in

Christ. This reframing is vital because we treat people from the overflow of our thought life. And that means we must view people through the lens of love if we're going to become ambassadors of forgiveness—people less bent toward being offended and more eager to bring the love, grace, and peace of Jesus with us everywhere we go.

Take some time to read the book of Philemon for yourself. Since it is short, you may want to read it more than once to help with comprehension and retention. Looking back at your video teaching notes from the beginning of this week may also be helpful as you work your way through this letter. Below you'll find notes to consider, space to record your own thoughts, and a few questions for you to answer.

Here are a few truths and themes you can look for as you read:

- Paul says he is a "prisoner" for Christ. The Greek meaning for this word δέσμιος (**desmios**) identifies that Paul is under custody and in prison. However, Paul uses this word to present a double meaning. While he is in prison, he is truly under the custody and will of Christ.[18]

- Paul refers to Onesimus as a bondservant. The original Greek word used here is δοῦλος (**doulos**) which is "pertaining to a state of being completely controlled by someone or something—'subservient to, controlled by.'"[19] So, here we see the connection between Paul and Onesimus. Paul, a prisoner (desmios), embodies a life of full surrender and loving service to his Savior and King. In a sense, Paul welcomes Onesimus from his former life as a bondservant (*doulos*) where he was controlled by others to his new life as a brother in Christ. Onesimus now shares in the same life of full surrender and loving service to King Jesus. This is the important truth Paul desires to communicate to Philemon.

- Paul wants Philemon to take his love for Paul and transfer it onto Onesimus and view him as a brother in Christ.

- When we place the wrongs others have committed against us into God's hands instead of holding those things against them, they can become ingredients in redemption.

- Paul is more concerned with changing Philemon's heart than forcing his actions.
- There needs to be a difference in how we as Christians see people and treat people and speak to people.

Use the space below to write out any thoughts or insights from your reading time, and then also answer the questions we've provided.

1. Which verses stood out the most to you?

2. What are some of your personal takeaways from this book of the Bible?

3. Paul wrote this letter to Philemon, using the basis of love to compel him to forgive. What if we viewed Jesus, the Word made flesh, as the Father's letter to us? And what if we considered the blood He spilled the purest of ink, declaring across the pages of history that we are forgiven and called to forgive? How might we feel more compelled to live out this message of forgiveness?

FIGURING OUT FORGIVENESS

Paul's approach to forgiveness in his letter to Philemon provides us with the basis for questions we can carry with us long after we close the pages of this study. You can jot down these questions in a personal journal to keep. You can fold down the corner of this page so you can come back here again and again. Whatever you need to do, commit to making these some of the questions you weave into keeping your heart swept clean as you continue to choose the ways of forgiveness all throughout your days. And go ahead and spend some time answering them today.

- Do I see the people involved as just a sum total of my earthly perspective of them or as Christ sees them?

- Do I see myself as the saint and them the sinner or that we are all humans in need of Christ?

- Do I want to force my agenda or appeal to people on the basis of love?

- Do I believe that even if they don't do the right thing that Christ can still redeem this situation in my life?

- Am I willing to accept God's version of the good that could possibly be worked out for all parties involved even if it doesn't feel good to me right now?

ENDNOTES

Week 1

1. Ludwig Koehler, Walter Baumgartner, et al., *The Hebrew and Aràmaic Lexicon of the Old Testament* (Leiden: E. J. Brill, 1994–2000), 409.

2. D. A. Carson, *The Gospel According to John*, The Pillar New Testament Commentary (Leicester, England; Grand Rapids, MI: W. B. Eerdmans, 1991), 348.

3. George R. Beasley-Murray, *John*, vol. 36, Word Biblical Commentary (Dallas: Word, Incorporated, 1999), 133.

Week 2

4. https://www.merriam-webster.com/dictionary/meditate.

5. https://www.merriam-webster.com/dictionary/ruminate.

6. Wendy Blight, *Hidden Joy in a Dark Corner* (Moody Publishers, 2009), 92.

7. William Arndt, et al., *A Greek-English Lexicon of the New Testament and Other Early Christian Literature* (Chicago: University of Chicago Press, 2000), 781.

Week 3

8. Ludwig Koehler, et al., *The Hebrew and Aramaic Lexicon of the Old Testament* (Leiden: E. J. Brill, 1994–2000), 666.

9. Steven C. Roy, "Embracing Social Justice: Reflections from the Storyline of Scripture," *Trinity Journal* 30, no. 1 (2009): 10–11.

10. Leon Morris, *The Gospel According to Matthew*, The Pillar New Testament Commentary (Leicester, England; Grand Rapids, MI: W. B. Eerdmans, 1992), 472. 28:2, 40–41.

11. C. H. Spurgeon, "Divine Forgiveness Admired and Imitated," in *The Metropolitan Tabernacle Pulpit Sermons*, vol. 31 (London: Passmore & Alabaster, 1885), 288.

Week 4

12. Walter L. Liefeld, *Ephesians*, vol. 10, The IVP New Testament Commentary Series (Downers Grove, IL: InterVarsity Press, 1997), Eph 4:31.

Week 5

13. Gerhard Kittel, Gerhard Friedrich, and Geoffrey William Bromiley, *Theological Dictionary of the New Testament* (Grand Rapids, MI: W. B. Eerdmans, 1985), 1000.

14. https://www.merriam-webster.com/dictionary/hope.

15. Ludwig Koehler, et al., *The Hebrew and Aramaic Lexicon of the Old Testament* (Leiden: E. J. Brill, 1994–2000), 692.

16. William Lee Holladay and Ludwig Köhler, *A Concise Hebrew and Aramaic Lexicon of the Old Testament* (Leiden: Brill, 2000), 178.

Week 6

17. https://www.merriam-webster.com/dictionary/ambassador.

18. Gerhard Kittel, Gerhard Friedrich, and Geoffrey William Bromiley, *Theological Dictionary of the New Testament* (Grand Rapids, MI: W. B. Eerdmans, 1985), 145.

19. Johannes P. Louw and Eugene Albert Nida, *Greek-English Lexicon of the New Testament: Based on Semantic Domains* (New York: United Bible Societies, 1996), 471.

LEADER'S GUIDE

Thanks for choosing the *Forgiving What You Can't Forget* video Bible study. Please take a few minutes to read this helpful information before you begin. It should answer most questions you may have. If you need a PDF version of this Leader's Guide, please go to: www.ForgivingWhatYouCantForget.com under Bible Study.

What Materials Are Needed for a Successful Group?

- Television monitor or screen
- DVD player*
- Six-session DVD with author Lysa TerKeurst*
- Watch or clock with which to monitor time
- One study guide for each group member (they will be writing in the study guide, so they will all need a copy)
- One copy of the book *Forgiving What You Can't Forget* for each group member (they will be reading the book between meetings, so they will all need a copy)
- Bible(s)
- Pen or pencil for each person

Note: You may purchase the videos to download or stream online instead of using the DVD. You can find the digital videos at Amazon.com, Vimeo.com /ondemand, Christianbook.com, or StudyGateway.com.

How Do I Prepare Before the Group Meets?

This video Bible study can work equally well in church and home groups. It is designed to adapt to groups of 90–120 minutes in length. The first thing you need to do is determine how much time your group has available to meet. Then look at the session outline for the session you will be leading. The outline shows suggested times for each section of the study, based on a 90-minute meeting (video times are exact; others are approximates). Depending on your group's specified meeting times, you can decide how you want to allocate your discussion and optional activity engagement.

If you have a group with limited time to meet each week, you can devote two meetings to each session in the study guide. In the second meeting, you can spend the time normally devoted to watching the video to discussing what you got out of the personal study and your reading of the book.

Viewing the video before your group meets will not only help you know what to expect but will help you select the questions in the study guide you want to include.

Make sure the room where you are viewing the video has chairs arranged so that everyone can see the screen. Then when it is time for group discussion, you may need to move chairs so that people in each discussion circle are facing each other. If your whole group will be discussing the material together, having chairs in a semicircle usually allows everyone to see the screen and one another's faces. If your group is large, we recommend that people divide into discussion circles of four to six people; arrange chairs accordingly.

Participants should read the introduction and chapters 1 and 2 of *Forgiving What You Can't Forget* before the first meeting and video teaching. Prior to each session in the study guide is a schedule of what participants can expect during the coming week. Please be sure to remind group members which chapters to read each week to prepare for the next teaching video. At the end of each personal study time in the study guide these instructions are repeated.

For some people, this study will be exactly what they need to walk them through a hard season or help them process a deep hurt. For others, this might only be the starting place for their healing. Please know there are some difficult realities that only a licensed Christian counselor will be able to help them navigate. At no point in this study should you ever feel the pressure to be someone's counselor. Below are some resources you can share with anyone in your group who is needing extra help.

Finding a counselor:

American Association of Christian Counselors: www.aacc.net
Focus on the Family: www.focusonthefamily.com

The Proverbs 31 Ministries Podcast: Therapy & Theology Series

Lysa TerKeurst created a podcast series with her personal, licensed professional counselor Jim Cress, as well as Proverbs 31 Ministries director of theology, Joel Muddamalle, that addresses topics such as forgiveness, boundaries, reconciliation, anxiety, and narcissism. There are also two episodes on pornography with licensed professional counselor Michael Cusick.

You can find all of these episodes on the official Proverbs 31 Ministries YouTube channel or the Proverbs 31 Ministries website.

SESSION 1

WHAT AM I SUPPOSED TO DO WITH ALL THE HURT?

Please have group members read the introduction and chapters 1 and 2 of *Forgiving What You Can't Forget* before this meeting.

As the leader, personally view the video before your group meets, and review the discussion questions in the study guide to prepare according to your group's time constraints.

Session Outline

Welcome (2–5 minutes)
Opening Reflection (10–15 minutes)

Video Teaching (25:30 minutes)

Group Discussion (40–45 minutes)

Closing (5 minutes)

Session Focus

What if forgiveness isn't supposed to be another hard thing we have to do? What if it's the necessary step to finally experience the peace we desperately want but can't get any other way? Forgiveness isn't a cruel command of God that makes light of the hurt people caused us. It's one of His most healing, crucial, and beautiful gifts. And it isn't made possible by our determination. Forgiveness is made possible by our cooperation with what God has already done for us. This week's teaching takes a close look at the story of Cain and Abel: the first time we see a human being having to make the choice between being ruled by bitterness and anger or surrendering those stirred-up emotions to God.

Session Tips

The "Welcome" is necessary only if you have group members who don't know each other. If your group is large, participants can introduce themselves to the people who will be in their smaller discussion circle.

The introduction and session one video segements are all part of session one.

SESSION 2

YOUR MIND, YOUR MOUTH, YOUR MASTER

Please have group members read chapters 3 and 4 of *Forgiving What You Can't Forget* before this meeting.

As the leader, personally view the video before your group meets, and go through the session in the study guide to choose the questions you want to cover.

Session Outline

Welcome and Opening Reflection (15–20 minutes)*

Video Teaching (21:30 minutes)
Group Discussion (40–45 minutes)
Closing (5 minutes)

*Note: You will see the Welcome and the Opening Reflection sections combined for the remainder of the sessions. Since you won't need to do introductions each week, you can feel free to use this time to open with prayer or you can go straight into discussion time.

Session Focus

Forgiveness shouldn't be so rare, and being constantly offended shouldn't be as common as it is. But for forgiveness to flow freely in our lives, we must learn to rule over the sin of our mind and our mouth with the strength of our Master. It's not wrong for us to feel strong emotions, but we must not let our emotions drive us to sin. This week, we'll learn not only how to have a marked moment of forgiveness, but we'll also discover what we can do when our emotions keep getting painfully triggered.

Session Tips

The "Opening Reflection" will take place in every session from now on. If you have a two-hour group, invite each person to share something. If you have a 90-minute group or less, you may not have time for everyone to share, so ask for some volunteers.

SESSION 3
THE DIVINE ECHO

Please have group members read chapters 5, 6, and 7 of *Forgiving What You Can't Forget* before this meeting.

As the leader, personally view the video before your group meets, and go through the session in the study guide to choose the questions you want to cover.

Session Outline

Welcome and Opening Reflection (15–20 minutes)

Video Teaching (27 minutes)
Group Discussion (40–45 minutes)
Closing (5 minutes)

Session Focus

God used dust and bone to make Adam and Eve, but that's not all they were. They were the very breath and touch of God - made in the image of God. As image bearers, they were designed to fill the earth with evidence of the goodness and glory of God. It's the same message God wants us to echo back and forth to one another today. Shame wants us to believe we are nothing more than what we've done. But shame is a tool of the enemy. That's why we must change how we see ourselves and others in order to make progress in this forgiveness journey. This week's video teaching will help us believe we are all made in the holy image of God, designed by God, and loved by God.

SESSION 4

THERE'S ALWAYS A MEANWHILE

Please have group members read chapters 8 and 9 of *Forgiving What You Can't Forget* before this meeting.

As the leader, personally view the video before your group meets, and go through the session in the study guide to choose the questions you want to cover.

Session Outline

Welcome and Opening Reflection (15–20 minutes)
Video Teaching (24 minutes)
Group Discussion (40–45 minutes)
Closing (5 minutes)

Session Focus

From pit to prison to palace, the long journey of Joseph rooted in the anger and unforgiveness from his brothers shows us that our physical reality is never the full story. With God, there is always a meanwhile. Along with the hurt and pain of what we can see in our physical reality, there is also the spiritual reality of how God is working all things together for our good and the good of others. This week's teaching will clearly remind us that we do not serve a do-nothing God. And even if we don't know how everything's going to turn out, we can know His goodness will be with us in the hardest moments and the longest days.

SESSION 5

THE COMPOUNDING EFFECT OF UNFORGIVENESS

Please have group members read chapters 10 and 11 of *Forgiving What You Can't Forget* before this meeting.

As the leader, personally view the video before your group meets, and go through the session in the study guide to choose the questions you want to cover.

Session Outline

Welcome and Opening Reflection (15–20 minutes)
Video Teaching (15 minutes)
Group Discussion (40–45 minutes)
Closing (5 minutes)

Session Focus

When we hear the story of Moses, we don't often connect it to the story of Joseph. But Moses and Joseph are very much connected. Turning back in Scripture to read about the hatred and unforgiveness of Joseph's brothers, we'll see the start of a chain of events that eventually leads to the nation of Israel being enslaved in Egypt. Enslavement God would one day use Moses to deliver them from. This week's teaching will help us see that unforgiveness doesn't just affect us. The choice not to forgive has a multiplied impact that extends far beyond what we will ever know. But if we'll willingly release everything that's hurtful into the hands of God, He'll be able to bring our healing full circle and help us live lives that are fruitful.

,ION 6

;N'T EASY, BUT IT IS GOOD

F. ᵴe have group members read chapters 12, 13, and 14 of *Forgiving What You Can't Forget* before this meeting.

As the leader, personally view the video before your group meets, and go through the session in the study guide to choose the questions you want to cover.

Session Outline

Welcome and Opening Reflection (15–20 minutes)
Video Teaching (21 minutes)
Group Discussion (40–45 minutes)
Closing (5 minutes)

Session Focus

Paul, who wrote the majority of the letters in the New Testament, is a true ambassador for Christ—a man trained to live the message of forgiveness. One of Paul's letters where he lives out this calling is in the book of Philemon. In this one-page letter, Paul demonstrates how forgiveness can begin when we choose to reframe how we see people using the eternal perspective of who they are in Christ. This reframing is vital because we treat people from the overflow of our thought life. And that means we must view people through the lens of love if we're going to become ambassadors of forgiveness ourselves—people less bent toward being offended and more eager to bring the love, grace, and peace of Jesus with us everywhere we go.

Session Tips

Remember: This is your last week of studying together! Feel free to do something to celebrate all the progress you've made as a group.

ABOUT THE AUTHOR

Lysa TerKeurst is the president of
Proverbs 31 Ministries and the #1 *New
York Times* bestselling author of *It's Not
Supposed to Be This Way, Uninvited, The
Best Yes,* and twenty-one other books.
But to those who know her best she's
just a simple girl with a well-worn Bible
who proclaims hope in the midst of good
times and heartbreaking realities.

Photograph by Kelsie Gorham

Lysa lives with her family in Charlotte, North Carolina.
Connect with her on a daily basis, see pictures of her family, and
follow her speaking schedule:

Website: www.LysaTerKeurst.com

**(Click on "events" to inquire about having
Lysa speak at your event.)**

Facebook: www.Facebook.com/OfficialLysa

Instagram: @LysaTerKeurst

Twitter: @LysaTerKeurst

If you enjoyed *Forgiving What You Can't Forget*, equip
yourself with additional resources at:

www.ForgivingWhatYouCantForget.com
www.Proverbs31.org

Proverbs 31
MINISTRIES

ABOUT PROVERBS 31 MINISTRIES

Lysa TerKeurst is the president of Proverbs 31 Ministries, located in Charlotte, North Carolina.

If you were inspired by *Forgiving What You Can't Forget* and desire to deepen your own personal relationship with Jesus Christ, we have just what you're looking for.

Proverbs 31 Ministries exists to be a trusted friend who will take you by the hand and walk by your side, leading you one step closer to the heart of God through:

> Free *First 5* Bible study app
> Free online daily devotions
> Online Bible studies
> Podcasts (You might find Lysa's Therapy and Theology
>   series very helpful as you continue your pursuit
>   of staying spiritually and emotionally healthy.)
> COMPEL Writer Training
> She Speaks Conference
> Books and resources

Our desire is to help you to know the Truth and live the Truth. Because when you do, it changes everything.

For more information about Proverbs 31 Ministries, visit

www.Proverbs31.org.

AN INVITATION FROM LYSA

When my family and I were trying to heal from the darkest season of our lives, I kept praying that we'd one day be able to use our experiences to help others find healing. But I didn't just want to do this at conferences. I've dreamed of inviting friends like you over to my home to break bread and share our broken hearts, face-to-face, heart-to-heart. So I'd love to invite you to Haven Place—a safe space for you to find the biblical and emotional healing you've been looking for.

If you'd like more information on the intimate gatherings, Bible studies, and retreats we'll be having here, such as:

- You, Me, and We: Stop Dancing with Dysfunction in Your Relationships
- Forgiving What You Can't Forget
- Moving On When Your Marriage Doesn't
- Practical seminars and intensives for those wanting to teach Bible studies with depth and clarity

. . . please visit lysaterkeurst.com/invitation-from-lysa.

I truly believe healing, hope, and forgiveness will be the anthem songs, prayers, and shouts of victory that will rise from this Haven Place.

FREE RESOURCES FOR YOU

For the days when forgiveness feels especially hard…

THE BEAUTY OF FORGIVING

Continue to be assured you can make progress on this journey with "The Beauty of Forgiving." Lysa wrote this personal and beautifully poetic encouragement just for you. Speak it out loud over yourself or hang it up in a place where you'll see it every day!

Visit https://proverbs31.org/forgiveness to download your copy today.

BIBLE STUDY EXERCISE WORKSHEETS

Deepen your understanding of what Scripture says about forgiveness and how it applies to your situation with printable worksheets to help you walk through the Bible study exercise from chapter 14.

Download your worksheets at https://proverbs31.org/forgiveness.

designed specifically

TO HELP YOU PROCESS WHAT YOU'RE LEARNING IN
FORGIVING WHAT YOU CAN'T FORGET

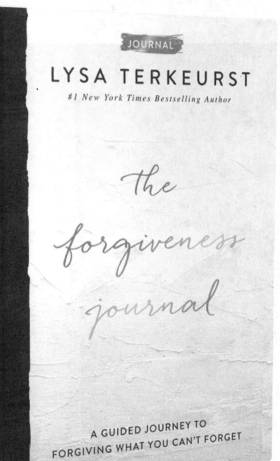

In this unique interactive journal, Lysa shares:

- Powerful readings about forgiveness and healing

- Key Scriptures for each chapter in *Forgiving What You Can't Forget*

- Journaling prompts with space to write

- Short prayers to start giving what you're working on to God

- Beautiful photographs of her home and other significant places she worked through her own healing

AVAILABLE WHERE BOOKS ARE SOLD

IF YOU ENJOYED THE CURRICULUM, MAKE SURE YOU DON'T MISS READING THE WHOLE BOOK.

Have you ever felt stuck in a cycle of unresolved pain, playing offenses over and over in your mind? You know you can't go on like this, but you don't know what to do next. Lysa TerKeurst has wrestled through this journey. But in surprising ways, she's discovered how to let go of bound-up resentment and overcome the resistance to forgiving people who aren't willing to make things right.

I FORGIVE

_____

FOR

_____

_____

_____

I FORGIVE

_____

FOR

_____

_____

_____

PERSON: _____

FACT: _____

IMPACT: _____

_____

_____

_____

_____

PERSON: _____

FACT: _____

IMPACT: _____

_____

_____

_____

I FORGIVE

_____

FOR

_____

_____

_____

I FORGIVE

_____

FOR

_____

_____

PERSON: _____

FACT: _____

IMPACT: _____

_____

_____

_____

_____

PERSON: _____

FACT: _____

IMPACT: _____

_____

_____

_____

I FORGIVE

_____

FOR

_____

_____

_____

I FORGIVE

_____

FOR

_____

_____

_____

PERSON: _____

FACT: _____

IMPACT: _____

_____

_____

_____

_____

PERSON: _____

FACT: _____

IMPACT: _____

_____

_____

_____

AND WHATEVER MY FEELINGS
DON'T YET ALLOW FOR,
THE BLOOD OF JESUS
WILL SURELY COVER.

AND WHATEVER MY FEELINGS
DON'T YET ALLOW FOR,
THE BLOOD OF JESUS
WILL SURELY COVER.

AND WHATEVER MY FEELINGS
DON'T YET ALLOW FOR,
THE BLOOD OF JESUS
WILL SURELY COVER.

AND WHATEVER MY FEELINGS
DON'T YET ALLOW FOR,
THE BLOOD OF JESUS
WILL SURELY COVER.